MARKETS AND IDEOLOGY IN THE CITY OF LONDON

Markets and Ideology in the City of London

David Lazar

Lecturer in Sociology
Goldsmiths' College, London

MACMILLAN

First published 1990

Published by
THE MACMILLAN PRESS LTD
Houndmills, Basingstoke, Hampshire RG21 2XS
and London
Companies and representatives
throughout the world

Typeset by Vine & Gorfin Ltd,
Exmouth, Devon

Printed in Hong Kong

British Library Cataloguing in Publication Data
Lazar, David, *1945–*
Markets and Ideology in the City of London
1. London (City). Financial institutions.
Sociological perspectives
I. Title
306'.342
ISBN 0–333–48983–7

To Jane

Contents

List of Tables

Acknowledgements

For reasons of confidentiality I am unable to name the firms, organisations and individuals in the City of London who generously gave up their time and took so much trouble to help me understand the City and those who work in it. I shall always remember my period in the City and the warmth with which I was (virtually always) treated. I am profoundly appreciative of this help.

I wish to thank my D.Phil. supervisor, Andrew Graham of Balliol College, Oxford. The structure of the book and many of the ideas it contains were developed in long conversations with him and in response to his remarkably insightful written comments. Michael Levin and Gerry Stimson, both of Goldsmiths' College, read countless drafts of all the chapters. For their enthusiastic support and advice – practical, intellectual and stylistic – I am deeply grateful. David Mackenzie, formerly of the University of Oxford Delegacy of Local Examinations, aided me enormously as I struggled to make sense of the schools attended by my interviewees. His knowledge of the English school system, past and present, must surely be unrivalled.

Jane Scott Paul made an enormous contribution to the project from start to finish. Her suggestions and criticisms have affected virtually every page of the book. Her enthusiasm for the project and her emotional and practical support were of immeasurable importance. For long periods she undertook an unreasonably high share of the housework. Now – at long last – the time has come for me to reciprocate!

I wish to record my gratitude to my colleagues in the Sociology Department at Goldsmiths' and to Goldsmiths' College for allowing me a year off to carry out the fieldwork. Finally, my students must not be forgotten: in the last few months they bore a share of the burden as the final revisions made me less energetic and probably less responsive than I normally try to be.

David Lazar

"Please don't disturb yourselves, my good people. My friend and I are only studying conditions among the rich."

1 Introduction

The very instability of the City was taken as a sign of its
sensitivity to real events, and as evidence of the adjusting power
inherent in free buying and selling. S. G. Checkland[1]

Individuals working in the financial markets of the City of London
are commonly believed to be exceptionally pro-market by British
standards. The subject of this book is the nature of these
pro-market views. How do these people perceive the financial
markets in which they work? What factors lead them to think as
they do? How do their experiences of financial markets affect their
perceptions of the proper relationship, in general, between the
state and the market?

Since the late 1970s the relationship between state and market
has been at the centre of public debate in the United Kingdom
and many other Western industrialised capitalist societies.
Political leaders across a wide spectrum, including even many
Marxists, have come to accept, to a greater extent than for a long
time, the efficacy of the market as a method of organising the
production and distribution of goods and services. We in the
West, and many societies in the rest of the world, are living
through a time when profound shifts of ideological commitment
are on the agenda: pro-market views are on the offensive. The
Keynesian ideology which successfully legitimated state
interventionism in most Western capitalist societies (the United
States being a major exception) during the 30 years after 1945 is
now either in retreat or holding the line with difficulty.

Yet, surprisingly, few sociologists have studied this pro-market
orientation which views the market – for which individuals and
firms produce and where buying and selling of a range of
commodities takes place – as virtually always the best
institutional solution to the problems of meeting the needs of
human beings. Since this pro-market orientation plays a crucial
role in many contemporary societies and may grow in importance,
it is essential to trace the manner in which the orientation
manifests itself in concrete situations. It is necessary also to
undertake research about the factors which produce and sustain
pro-market views. The present work is a contribution to this task.

The immediate object of concern is a sector of the British political economy where strong pro-market views are predominant. It is commonly held that those who work in the City of London financial markets – City people – believe passionately in the absolute and general superiority of the market mechanism over alternative systems for allocating or distributing goods and services. City people are (especially by British standards) strongly pro-market.[2] The City provides us with a fruitful site to study the relationship between market and state.

It is essential to establish that City people do believe in the market but it is necessary to go beyond this point. Three subsidiary questions are raised. First, what do City people mean by a belief in the market? In other words, in what sense or senses do they believe in the market? Second, why do City people believe in the market? Third, what are the implications of their belief in the market? Each question is discussed briefly below and explored further in later chapters.

Much of what is written in later chapters about a belief in the market and pro-market ideologies should be seen in the broader context of British social development since the Second World War. This Introduction therefore ends with a discussion of the main features of the relationship between the market and the state in the United Kingdom since 1945.

1 THE CITY VIEW OF FINANCIAL MARKETS AND THE MARKET MECHANISM IN GENERAL

What do City people mean when they refer to the superiority of the market over alternative mechanisms? Two issues are involved: (a) their conception of financial 'markets'; and (b) their tendency to generalise about markets and economies on the basis of their knowledge of *one* kind of market (financial markets).

(a) The City view of financial markets

In the City view, financial markets are characterised by the direct, immediate relationship of market participants to market forces.[3] Financial markets are what economists call flex-price markets: they are markets in which some commodity has to be cleared (for example, securities, bank balances) and prices change constantly to adjust the relationship between supply and demand. In this respect financial markets are like the stall of a street-market trader who wishes to sell everything by the end of the day: prices must be adjusted constantly to achieve this aim.

The time horizon of participants in financial markets is very short because there are no time lags in financial markets: the commodities already exist (for instance, company securities) or can be produced very quickly (for instance, traded option contracts can be written on demand). In both street and financial markets, participants are constantly changing prices or reacting to changing prices (equity prices, interest rates, and so on) in a very immediate fashion.

This point is illustrated in the following example from an interview with an institutional salesman in the pre-Big Bang Gilt-edged (that is, government or government-guaranteed) securities market. He explained that because the market moves very fast, there is never time to telephone more than a few institutional fund managers if you spot an opportunity to sell before the market falls:

> You [the dealer and fund managers -DL] can only make so many decisions before the market changes . . . The jobbers aren't stupid: they'll change prices against you. If they know full well that there's a piece of news – the market's going to fall -they'll just whip away the bids from you [i.e., lower their buying price] at the right time. You get in – that piece of news is worth half a point of the market – and it's already happened – you haven't even dealt!

Consequently, market participants are obliged to act fast. Furthermore, they have to take a short-term view:

> And most of our [Gilt Department's] half-an-hour's chat in the morning to start with is geared to what the market is going to do today. Whereas you get people like [the Department's economist] who sit down and work out where they think the market will be in a year or two years time. . . . People like [the economist] sort of glibly sit down and write, with the known facts they've got their two or three year view of the market which can be shot to ribbons. You get something like a quadrupling in the price of oil and all their prognostications are absolutely worthless. So the fund manager actually sits down

and talks to me on a daily basis . . . So that all your views are very, very short-term.[4]

In other words, City people are geared to immediate responses to market forces and they believe that financial markets efficiently balance supply and demand for funds, securities, currencies or whatever by frequent changes of prices.

(b) The City view of markets in general

City people assume that all needs are best met through the market mechanism: that we must trust in competitive markets to attain a balance between supply and demand at reasonable prices. Even those individuals who lack the cash to translate needs into effective demand are best served by the market – where necessary earnings can be supplemented or replaced by cash handouts from the taxpayer. City people believe that attempts to substitute some other arrangement for the market are almost always inefficient and may lead to disaster. In other words, they assume that the model of how financial markets function can be generalised without exception to all markets and economic sectors. This belief in the general applicability of the financial market model can take extreme forms. After his interview, a young participant in the international capital markets said that African peasants faced by falling prices for their commodity should switch to production of another commodity. The interviewer suggested that they might not have the means to do so. 'Oh', he said, 'I hadn't thought of that'.

However, this assumption that the City person's experience of financial markets can be generalised runs into intractable difficulties once we realise that there are (a) different kinds of markets and (b) different kinds of competition. Let us take each point in turn. Financial markets are flex-price markets as noted above, that is, prices change constantly to clear the market of commodities (for example, equities, funds available for borrowers, foreign exchange). Prices can change constantly and often at great speed because these markets do not involve massive investment in plant, raw materials and labour over a long period. Product markets operate altogether differently because massive, long-term investment (plant, technology, labour over a long period) has to be recouped once the products are available. Prices in product markets are 'fixed' because costs have to be recovered – if they cannot be, the firm will stop producing the line or will move to a lower level of capacity utilisation at the fixed price. Because product markets cannot be organised around continuously changing prices they cannot work as financial markets do. The attempt to generalise the experience of financial markets to all sectors is unsatisfactory and misleading because it fails to distinguish between flex-price and fixed-price markets.

Furthermore, the City view is subject to a second criticism because it assumes that all markets involve the same kind of competition. Of course, all firms and individuals in whatever market fear being wiped out by competitors but competition in financial markets and product markets is very different. Competition between investors (and between investment advisors) in financial markets takes the form primarily of arbitrage: the participant sees a difference between the price or return in one market and in another (for example, New York versus Tokyo) and takes advantage of the discrepancy; or the investor will note that equities in company A provide a better return on investment (at a given level of risk) than those in company B; or, the investor may sell certain equities and buy particular government securities to achieve a higher rate of capital growth. The decisions made by investors to move their funds between markets, different securities of a similar type (for instance, equities) or between different investment vehicles (for instance, from equities to government securities) are all examples of the general rule that investors in financial markets seek the best return at a given level of risk and will switch investments to achieve this aim. Market-makers in financial markets (for example, jobbers before 'Big Bang'), unlike investors, do not make money by investing capital but by the spread between 'bid' (buying) and 'offer' (selling) prices. The market-maker therefore needs to clear 'positions' (that is, holdings) in particular lines so that capital is not tied up in financing 'positions'. Instead, capital finances dealing which is where market-makers generate their profits. Dealing involves responding to short-term changes in the balance between supply and demand: this is why the logic of market-making is a short-term logic.

Competition in product markets takes a distinctly different form because long-term, massive investment is essential. Such competition is bound up with what Joseph Schumpeter[5] called 'creative destruction'. Firms invest in new technology and plant over long time spans for fear of their destruction if they fail to do so. Product markets constantly revolutionise themselves in terms of technology, plant, objects produced and so on. Competition is in terms of how things are produced and what is produced rather than being mainly about changing prices constantly.

Ultimately, the difference between financial and product markets, whether we view them from the point of view of types of markets or types of competition, comes down to the matter of time-horizons. Product markets necessarily involve longer time lags. This provides us with an insight into why the City takes the short-term view: financial markets work in this way and City people judge all else by the criteria with which they are familiar. City people have good reason to believe that financial markets do work efficiently as markets for securities, and so on, but they illegitimately generalise their experience to all markets. The City view that all markets can work effortlessly without state intervention derives from the erroneous view that the world can be treated like a very big stock exchange.

2   WHY CITY PEOPLE BELIEVE IN THE MARKET

Why do City people believe in the market? One answer is that they believe in the market because their experience as participants in particular financial markets has helped to convince them that the market mechanism is competitive[6] and works efficiently. Chapter 3 documents the power of financial markets to influence and constrain the individuals who work in them. To a large degree, markets force one to behave in certain ways if one wishes to achieve specific aims; this applies to individuals and enterprises. Belief in the market is both a result of the experience of working in apparently efficient and competitive financial markets and a necessity if one is to sustain the required motivation to be effective in an intense and volatile working environment. After all, how can one sustain the requisite motivation unless one believes in the claims made for markets by enthusiastic pro-marketeers? What is striking about the evidence presented in chapter 3 is the positive commitment both to their jobs and the market which participants articulated in interviews.

However, City people do not begin their careers with neutral views about the market, with a subsequent shift to pro-market views as a result of their experience of financial markets. Usually, it appears, City people begin their careers with strong pro-market orientations. Indeed, it seems that they are attracted to the City because they see it as the epitome of free competition. What happens afterwards, therefore, reinforces and reproduces a powerful predisposition to approve of markets as the solution to virtually all problems of supplying goods and services.

It should not be assumed that City people are free to make up their own minds about the virtues of the market. This is by no means the case. Recruits and established participants are faced by insidious pressures to conform ideologically. Participants in financial markets are expected to evince extraordinarily positive views about the market and private ownership. It is difficult, to say the least, to survive and prosper in the City if one dissents on matters which are effectively fundamental tenets of City life. The few socialists encountered during the research were exceptionally strong-minded and reflective individuals; even such individuals find the going tough. It is notable that none of them were thoroughgoing left-wingers.

Some ideologically deviant individuals presumably decide to leave the City. Future research on those who do would be valuable. In the absence of such data, one must rely upon the testimony of those who remain and shut up (or keep rather quiet). Some evidence on this issue of the intolerance of City culture is presented in chapter 4: the conclusion drawn is that normally a challenge to the predominant pro-market views would be dangerous to one's career.

The overall result is that within the City dissenting voices are seldom heard. At times, it seemed as if interviewees were incapable of even understanding how anyone could be sceptical about markets. Furthermore, outside critics are written off as individuals who either do not understand financial (and other) markets or are opposed to capitalism and, therefore, deeply prejudiced. At the end of the day, City people live in a comfortable and closed ideological world where their prejudices and misunderstandings about how markets work and how state intervention intersects with market processes need never be confronted.

In addition to the prior pro-market orientations of City recruits, the power of markets to mould individuals, and the ideologically closed character of City life, two other factors contribute to the creation and sustenance of a strong belief in the market. The first is the material incentive to conform: City salaries are extraordinarily high relative to comparable jobs outside the City and everyone interviewed believed that this trend was bound to continue. Salaries of £50 000 to £100 000 – frequently for not especially senior posts – are a powerful incentive to still any doubts about markets.

Second, the domination of the City by particular social classes[7] – commercial and landed interests – is an important factor explaining the pro-market views of City individuals. The City has always been dominated by the wealthy and the wealthy favour markets and private ownership. Individuals who work in the City are, as explained earlier, expected to conform rigidly on this score. The majority of interviewees grew up in fairly privileged backgrounds and such origins are connected to pro-market beliefs: such individuals have no difficulty in fitting in. However, and this is a matter of some importance and it will be discussed in chapter 4, even those from modest backgrounds (around a quarter of interviewees) are remarkably pro-market. Consequently, social class background cannot on its own explain the pro-market orientation of those individuals who decide to work in the City.

In summary, City life is characterised by a powerful consensus about the virtues of the market and the iniquities of efforts to use state intervention to alter market processes or outcomes. This consensus is seldom challenged for a number of reasons. First, recruits enter the city with robust pro-market views. To some degree this pro-market orientation is a consequence of the privileged social class background of many recruits. However, four factors internal to the City are clearly significant. The ideological consensus is sustained by (a) the experience of working in markets, (b) the closed character of City culture, (c) the material incentives to conform and (d) the traditional domination of the City by commercial and landed interests with pronounced pro-market views and a strong antipathy to public ownership.

3   THE IMPLICATIONS OF THE CITY BELIEF IN THE MARKET

One implication has already been mentioned: a tendency to take the short-term view. This tendency is a consequence of working in volatile financial markets and then, erroneously, generalising the lessons learnt to all markets. There is a second implication which is of equal importance. The City's virtually absolute preference for the market solutions leads to certain pronounced opinions about key socio-economic issues. In interviews the following were discussed: privatisation (that is, selling off of publicly-owned assets), progressive income taxation (that is, a graduated income taxation system) and, finally, but not in all interviews, government policy on unemployment.

Interviewees articulated strikingly similar views on these matters: enormous and, on the whole, enthusiastic support for the British government's privatisation policy; widespread doubts about, and in many cases outright opposition to, the mildly progressive income taxation system of 1985; little sympathy for state expenditure to reduce high unemployment. In each case, City views were (and are) out of step with British public opinion. At the end of the day, City people adhere almost always to pro-market ideologies.

4 STATE AND MARKET IN BRITAIN SINCE 1945

The inclination of City people to hold strong pro-market views has been noted. The relationship between the market and the state assumes crucial significance for City people – as for many others in Britain – because state intervention increased steadily in Britain after 1945, as it did in the other advanced capitalist societies. Many have come to see such intervention as a threat. The ideologies of those who work in the city have developed in the context of a debate about the legitimacy of state intervention.

In the United Kingdom, from 1945 until the late 1970s, it was acccepted by the major political parties (Conservative, Labour and Liberal) that the state should – and, indeed, had to – play a major part in economic affairs and social policy. This agreement about the fundamental features of British society is sometimes referred to as the post-war 'consensus' or 'settlement'.[8] Essentially, it was agreed that the state should discharge three general roles:

(a) an economic role as regulator of the economy in conformity with Keynesian theories about the management of aggregate demand to achieve full employment;

(b) an economic role as owner of certain basic industries which, in some cases, were unattractive to private investors because they generated little or no profit;

(c) a welfare role, either providing goods or services directly to those in need (National Health Service, council housing, and so on) or providing the means to purchase these in the Market (social security payments of various kinds).

The first and second roles entailed a combination of market and state intervention often referred to as the 'mixed economy'; the activities associated with the third role are usually summed up by the term 'the welfare state'. The three roles are briefly examined below with particular attention to pro-market criticism of state intervention inspired by writers associated with the *Institute of Economic Affairs* and specifically by F. A. Hayek and Milton Friedman.[9] Powerful criticisms of the welfare state and mixed economy have been developed by Marxists[10] but these have not had any impact upon City people. Consequently, this type of attack on the post-war consensus is not examined here.

During the period of consensus, state regulation of the economy was backed by the Keynesian belief that the market could not, without assistance from state intervention, guarantee steady economic growth and full employment.[11] Economic policy under both Conservative and Labour governments was based on attempts to manipulate the level of aggregate demand in the economy in order to achieve full employment: this involved government budget deficits at times, high levels of state spending[12] and continuous state intervention in the economy. State intervention went beyond demand management to include regulation and intervention across a wide field: incomes policy, regional policy and so on. Indeed, William Beveridge – like Keynes, a major influence on the developing post-war consensus – predicted the great increase in state intervention which he saw as an inescapable accompaniment of the search for full employment. In his *Full Employment in a Free Society*, written during the years of the Second World War, he wrote:[13]

> Full employment cannot be won and held without a great extension of the responsibilities and powers of the state exercised through organs of the central government.

Pro-market criticism of state interventionism always existed but, between 1945 and the mid-1970s, it was (at least in the case of British politics) a fringe phenomenon.

From the mid-1970s, criticism both of Keynesian demand management and of the machinery of state intervention became both more strident and more widespread. Under a Labour government, in the second half of the 1970s, control of inflation and public expenditure assumed priority and the pursuit of full employment was less emphasised. After 1979, the transformation was complete: the new Conservative government stoutly rejected the view that governments could achieve full employment using Keynesian demand management techniques; instead, control of inflation became the over-riding government goal.[14]

Throughout the 30-year period when the post-war consensus was substantially unchallenged, it was accepted that the state should, or had to, own and run certain enterprises or industries.[15] There was, of course, disagreement both within and between political parties about whether any particular industry should be under private or public ownership – in the parlance of critics of public ownership, the latter is termed 'state ownership'. Such disputes affected Steel, Shipbuilding, Aircraft manufacture, and the like. But there was always an acceptance that certain basic industries should be publicly-owned (for example: railways, the telephone network, British Airways, gas, electricity, water). This consensus about the legitimacy of public ownership of certain industries came under increasing attack from the strongly pro-market critics of state intervention,[16] most prominently from the Conservative Party under Mrs Thatcher, during the second half of the 1970s.

Hostility to public ownership culminated in the 'privatisation' programme of the post-1979 Conservative governments. The assumption underlying what is in fact a 'denationalisation' policy ('denationalisation' because it removes industries from public ownership) is that the state should run few if any industries because private ownership combined with the market will always be more efficient at meeting the needs of individuals and because state intervention invariably diminishes (individual) freedom. Antipathy to the institutions of state intervention is a keynote of the Conservative government's approach: the policies of deregulation of industry[17] and privatisation of publicly-owned firms (selling shares in these firms to private shareholders) have been vigorously pursued. The basic assumption of the government has been that the state should 'interfere' in the workings of the market only in exceptional circumstances.

During the period of consensus, the welfare state was regarded as a desirable and inevitable institutional feature of British society.[18] The market, it was assumed, not only could not deal with all the needs of people but, in fact, itself often created problems which needed a response from the state. People on low earnings might need subsidised private housing or direct provision of council housing; the chronically ill might need permanent support from the community; industrial decline and technological change might result in unemployment for particular groups which could quite reasonably expect support and retraining from the community. Above all, the National Health Service, through which the state provided health care virtually or actually free at the point of delivery, was strongly supported by all the major political parties. However, the pro-market critics of state intervention – including the welfare state – grew in influence in the second half of the 1970s and in the early 1980s as disillusion with the consensus became more widespread and the proponents of state intervention and welfare lost some of their long-standing confidence as a result of the increasing difficulties of the British economy.

Critics of the welfare state claimed that it had spawned a network of inefficient and paternalist bureaucratic agencies which were a drain on national resources and undermined self-reliance and individual freedom. This latter point – the destruction of self-help – is especially significant because it implies that the welfare state is constantly creating more problems. Milton and Rose Friedman[19] articulate the core of the pro-market case against the welfare state:

> Most of the present welfare programmes should never have been enacted. If they had not been, many of the people now dependent on them would have become self-reliant individuals instead of wards of the state.

In summary, the dominant view for about three decades after 1945 was that state intervention in the forms of regulation of the economy, ownership of basic industries, and provider of a wide range of welfare services was desirable and inevitable. From the mid-1970s pro-market criticisms of state intervention became both more strident and more effective as British society entered a period of profound economic and social crisis.

5   THE STRUCTURE OF THE STUDY

The structure of the study is as follows: chapter 2 analyses interview data relevant to the question, 'Do City people believe in the market?'. It also provides data about the City conception of the market. The final section advances evidence in favour of the argument that the pro-market views of the interviewees were atypical of British public opinion at the time of the fieldwork (1985).

Chapter 3 investigates the subjective meaning of markets for City people to aid understanding of both how the market appears to them in their daily lives and of what a 'belief in the market' as an institution means for such individuals. Section 2 of the chapter includes a very brief discussion of an important issue: the origin of the City's tendency to take a short-term view of the economy and industry. The origin lies in the volatile nature of financial markets within which, in consequence, one can only have short-term strategies. The short-term view of industry and economy is a result of the pro-market views of the City combined with a generalisation of the financial market model to all markets and economic sectors.

Chapter 4 tackles the issues of how to explain the City belief in markets. First, it is likely that recruits enter the City with strong pro-market views. Second, the idea that such views are merely the result of privileged social class backgrounds is criticised on the grounds that many participants in the markets do not come from such backgrounds and that recruits to City career posts from all social class backgrounds manifest an exceptional predisposition (by British standards) to approve of market solutions to nearly every problem. Third, the chapter examines the practical working context which nourishes pro-market beliefs. A working experience of financial markets is a crucial factor reinforcing and reproducing vigorous pro-market views. Finally, the chapter examines the deeply intolerant nature of City ideology and the resulting virtual absence of dissent.

Chapter 5 tackles the implication in the realm of ideology of the pro-market views of interviewees. The implication is the dominance of pro-market ideologies, close to or coincident with Neo-liberalism. The chapter presents data about the ideologies of interviewees.

Chapter 6 takes up the issue of how City recruits are socialised into City culture, a culture dominated by complacent and vigorous pro-market views. The main factors referred to include: the strong influence of participation in a financial market on how individuals view markets in general as a means to organise production and allocate goods and services; the material incentive to adopt pro-market views; the everyday informal pressures to conform to a very narrow range of acceptable conduct and ideas; the intolerance of City culture to dissent on the issue of the general applicability of the market principle.

Chapter 7 summarises the conclusions of the various chapters and examines the implications of this research for future sociological work. Three points in particular should be noted. First, we know little about the genesis of the pro-market orientation. Second, sociological knowledge of how markets, other than labour markets, operate is scanty. Third, despite the recent crop of sociological books and articles summarising recent research on popular opinions about socio-political issues, sociologists have little of an empirical nature to say about the concrete manifestations and origins of ideologies. Fourth, the research may have implications for our understanding of the radical right in Britain. A major argument of the study is that, in financial markets, exposure to brutal, but apparently 'efficient' market forces, is an important factor encouraging and reproducing strong pro-market views. On the basis of this argument, a tentative hypothesis is developed about the strategy of Mrs Thatcher's government. The hypothesis is that this strategy is based less than is often thought on the battle to change ideas directly; instead, it should be conceived as, to a large degree, an attempt to change the ideology of British people by fundamentally altering the economic context within which individuals operate. More specifically, government policy is based, implicitly and at times explicitly, on the reasoning that exposure to relatively unregulated market forces will fundamentally affect the behaviour, values and ideas of large numbers of individuals. Viewed in this light, the Thatcher government is engaged to a greater degree than is commonly supposed in an exercise of an economic determinist kind!

NOTES

1.   S. G. Checkland, 'The Mind of the City 1870–1914', *Oxford Economic Papers* (New Series), ix, 1957: p. 270. The terminology of the financial markets is explained in Appendix 3.
2.   In this study strong pro-market views are sometimes referred to as 'a belief in the market'.
3.   Checkland, in 'The Mind of the Market' (p. 265), writing about the period 1870–1914 asserts of the City that 'the mass of its operators were the prisoners of immediacy'. My attention was drawn to this quotation by G. Ingham's *Capitalism Divided?* (p. 242).
4.   Taped interview: 136.
5.   J. Schumpeter, *Capitalism, Socialism and Democracy*, chapter 7.
6.   The existence of competition is critical to the case for markets. City people have usually turned a blind eye to restrictions on competition in their own particular financial market. They do, however, often notice restrictions in other parts of the City.

Competition in markets, including financial markets, is often restricted deliberately but restrictions can also be a result of economic or other changes. Here only deliberate restriction is examined; unintentional restriction of competition (for example, the decline in the number of jobbing firms) is discussed in Appendix 3. In *Economy and Society*, Weber distinguishes between 'open' and 'closed' groups (pp. 43–6). Weber was interested in the way in which groups close off, wholly or partially, membership in order to restrict access to the advantages they enjoy. Such more-or-less 'closed' groups use various means of exclusion including rules, required educational qualifications, class or status membership. Those inside the group may, indeed, compete freely (although this is not always either the case or the aim) but outsiders are prevented from doing so. Weber, in fact, explicitly mentioned financial markets in this connection (p. 45):

> Thus a caste, a guild, or a group of stock exchange brokers, which is closed to outsiders, may allow to its members a perfectly free competition for all the advantages which the group as a whole monopolizes for itself.

For discussion of the concept of social closure, see: F. Parkin, 'Strategies of Social Closure in Class Formation' in Parkin (ed.), *The Social Analysis of Class Structure*; Parkin, *Marxism and Class Theory*: Part 1, chapters 1–3.

Restrictions on competition have long been a deliberately constructed feature of City life: thus, for example, stockbroking firms have competed fiercely with each other but have until recently excluded many potential competitors (for example, banks and foreign-owned firms) from membership of The Stock Exchange. Ingham makes the general point (*Capitalism Divided?*: p. 87):

> . . . the City has constantly striven to erect non-economic barriers to entry since the mid-nineteenth century, through the establishment of

exclusive associations based upon the discount houses, the accepting houses, the Stock Exchange and Lloyds.

Lisle-Williams focuses on barriers to free competition in the English merchant banking sector and states that many of these restrictions are rapidly disappearing. His 'A sociological analysis of changing social organization and market conduct in the English merchant banking sector' (University of Oxford D.Phil. thesis, 1982) examines the reciprocal effects of social relations and market forces. Two broad questions guided the research:

(a) How do social relations and the cultural milieu modify the impact of market forces?
(b) How does economic change affect the normative framework of market activity?' (Abstract of thesis, no pagination)

He states (p. 1):

The distinctive contribution of this study, compared with research in economics and economic history, is that it systematically examines the social and cultural context of merchant banking and traces the influence of this context on financial activity.

The core of the thesis (chapters 4 and 5) is his analysis of the (upper class) community of merchant banking and how this has affected market behaviour. In an article which draws upon the thesis Lisle-Williams surveys the achievement of considerable unity among the merchant banking dynasties and the 'incorporation of merchant banking families into the upper stratum' ('Merchant banking dynasties in the English class structure: ownership, solidarity and kinship in the City of London, 1850–1960', *BJS*, xxxv, No. 3, September 1984: p. 338). In a second article, also based upon the thesis, he develops an explanation of the long survival of family ownership in English merchant banking. The close community of merchant banking facilitated 'widespread agreement about the limits to competition and the desirability of mutual aid as a strategy for collective survival'. ('Beyond the market: the survival of family capitalism in the English merchant banks', *BJS*, xxxv, No. 2, June 1984: p. 245).

He traces the history of merchant banking between 1850 and 1960 and shows that the Bank of England played a crucial role in underpinning the merchant banking system during difficult times. Indeed during the long years of stagnation in the sector from the inter-war period until the late 1950s, such co-opeation was 'a rational strategy' (ibid.: p. 262) and, in fact, such co-operation exemplifies the fundamental point made in his thesis that the social organisation of the merchant banking community mediated the impact of economic forces. He formulates this point clearly in the conclusion to his D.Phil. thesis (p. 321):

The most important finding was that as a result of informal and official arrangements, private [as opposed to corporate – DL] ownership was protected from the worst effects of market forces and from takeovers by "outsiders".

Yet, in the long run, market forces have triumphed over small and often relatively inefficient family firms because these firms could not compete effectively in the international capital markets of the 1960s and beyond. Much of the thesis analyses (p. 317):

> the replacement of family-based ownership and control, personalized domination, patronage, and small-scale organization in the merchant banking sector by a more institutionalized, bureaucratic mode of organization.

Needless to say, City people see controls on entry somewhat differently from Ingham and Lisle-Williams: they focus on the need to protect standards through careful scrutiny of the qualifications (capital, skills, personal attributes) of individuals and firms seeking entry to the City markets. For a brief discussion of the recent weakening of City restrictive practices, see Appendix 3 of the present study.

7.   For example, see: R. Whitley's 'The City and Industry: the directors of large companies, their characteristics and connections' in P. Stanworth and A. Giddens (eds), *Elites and Power in British Society*: pp. 65–80. Whitley provides evidence about the privileged educational backgrounds of members of City élites. Of 106 directors of merchant banks and discount houses for whom information was available (no data for 50): 84 went to private (fee-paying schools); of these 84, 57 went to the most prestigious Public Schools – Eton, Harrow, Winchester, Rugby, Charterhouse, Marlborough; indeed, 45 of the 84 went to Eton, Harrow or Winchester. J. Scott's *The Upper Classes: Property and Privilege in Britain* (p. 80) and the article by Lisle-Williams about merchant banking dynasties mentioned in the preceding note are evidence of the social unity of the powerful wealthy families who held sway in the City for so long. Today, the City is increasingly dominated by giant banks and financial conglomerates rather than by wealthy families.

8.   Andrew Gamble refers to 'the social democratic Keynesian consensus': see 'The Free Economy and the Strong State' in R. Miliband and J. Saville (eds), *The Socialist Register 1979*, p. 21. Bob Jessop writes about 'the economic and political settlement between capital and labour': see 'The Transformation of the State in Post-war Britain' in R. Scase (ed.), *The State in Western Europe*: p. 28. See also: Shirley Williams, *Politics is for People*: p. 18; Ian Gilmour, *Inside Right*: pp. 19–21.

9.   References to Friedman's and Hayek's writings are provided below. For further examples of pro-market criticisms of state intervention and welfare services, see: R. Harris and A. Seldon, *Over-Ruled on Welfare: The increasing desire for choice in education and medicine and its frustration by 'representative' government*; R. Boyson (ed.), *1985: An escape from Orwell's 1984*: Introduction and chapters 2, 3 and 5.

10.   See, for instance: J. Westergaard and H. Resler, *Class in a Capitalist Society*: Part 1, section 5; Part 2, chapter 5; Part 3, chapters 3 and 4; I. Gough, *The Political Economy of the Welfare State*: especially, chapters 3 and 7.

11.   This discussion of Keynesian demand management is based mainly on: P. Donaldson, *10 x Economics*: chapters 1 and 2; P. Donaldson, *A Question of*

Economics: chapter 3–5; G. Bannock *et al.*, *The Penguin Dictionary of Economics:* pp. 251–3; G. Dalton, *Economic Systems and Society*: pp. 101–6.

12. Useful discussions of the trend of public expenditure can be found in: I. Gough, *The Political Economy of the Welfare State*: chapter 5; P. Donaldson, *10 x Economics*: chapter 3, especially pp. 56–7. See also I. Gough's 'State Expenditure in Advanced Capitalism' (particularly section 11), *New Left Review*, No. 92, July–August 1973. A. T. Peacock and J. Wiseman's *The Growth of Public Expenditure in the United Kingdom* provides figures showing total government expenditure as a percentage of Gross National Product (GNP) for the period from 1890–1955: see Appendix, Table A-6 (p. 166). Figures up to 1984–85 for general government expenditure as a percentage of Gross Domestic Product (GDP) were presented in a statement issued by The Treasury on 12 November 1985 and reprinted in full in the *Financial Times* on the following day (13 November 1985). These latter figures show the figure as 43 per cent in 1978–79, reaching a peak of 46.5 per cent in 1982–83 and at 45.5 per cent in 1984–85 (the fieldwork on which the present study is based was carried out in the first half of 1985).

13. Beveridge, *Full Employment in a Free Society*: p. 36, para. 44.

14. See: A. Gamble, 'Economic Policy' (p. 140) in H. Drucker and others (eds), *Developments in British Politics*; P. Donaldson, *A Question of Economics*: p. 46.

15. See, for example: I. Gilmour, *Inside Right*: 'Post-War Conservatism' (esp., p. 19); C. A. R. Crosland, *The Future of Socialism*: chapters XVIII–XX. Gilmour is a Conservative who is still attached to the main elements of the post-war consensus; Crosland was a leading exponent of consensus politics within the Labour Party. Marxists, although deeply critical of the consensus for sustaining rather than fundamentally changing Western societies, assumed, like supporters of the consensus, that state interventionism was here to stay. Ralph Miliband, writing in the late 1960s, stated:

> . . . the scale and pervasiveness of state intervention in contemporary capitalism is now immeasurably greater than ever before, and will undoubtedly continue to grow; and much the same is also true for the vast range of social services for which the state in these societies has come to assume direct or indirect responsibility. (*The State in Capitalist Society*: p. 9).

16. See, for example: R. Lewis, 'Denationalization' in R. Boyson (ed.), *1985: An escape from Orwell's 1984*: pp. 19–28. Lewis quotes from the Conservative Party's 1974 *Campaign Guide* (produced during Edward Heath's leadership of the party) and criticises it for accepting the mixed economy. He is especially incensed by the statement that the party has never believed that 'the issue of nationalisation or denationalisation is a matter to be decided on doctrinaire grounds.' For Lewis, denationalisation (nowadays called 'privatisation') is a matter of principle and he links this to the 'observation that concentration of power is detrimental to freedom' (pp. 20–1).

17. The government presented its record on 'deregulation' of industry up to 1985 in United Kingdom Cabinet Office, *Lifting the Burden*: see chapter 1 and Annex 1. Note in particular the statement (p. 3, para. 1.12):

'Deregulation has been a continuing priority of the Government since 1979 and much has already been achieved'. According to the *Financial Times* (21 May 1985), the government had already raised £17.2bn through public asset sales since 1979 when it came to office. This figure includes sales of local authority assets (mainly council houses) and firms privatised by the government. The government momentum in the matter of privatisation has increased since then (British Gas, liquidation of the remaining public stake in BP, and so on) with many privatisation issues in prospect (Electricity, Water, and more).

18.   Once again, the writings of Gilmour and Crosland can be treated as expressions of the post-war consensus view: I. Gilmour, *Inside Right*: esp. p. 19; C. A. R. Crosland, *The Future of Socialism*: Part 3.

19.   M. and R. Friedman, *Free to Choose*: p. 149. For a critical review of the pro-market or Neo-liberal standpoint on welfare, see: R. Mishra, *The Welfare State in Crisis*: pp. 30–46.

2 The City, Markets and the State

1 INTRODUCTION

This chapter examines the question 'Do City people believe in the market?'. To what extent do individuals working in the City hold strong pro-market views? Nearly a hundred interviews[1] were carried out between mid-February and late-July 1985. Interviewees were asked questions about the issues of privatisation, progressive income tax and state policy on unemployment. Each of these issues explores the views of interviewees about the desirable relationship between the state and the market even though none is explicitly a question about markets. It will be argued in this introductory section that questions about the above issues (privatisation, progressive income taxation, unemployment policy) do tap interviewees' views about the desirable balance between market processes and state intervention. Furthermore, data presented in the chapter will show how each topic is in effect treated by interviewees as a question about the role of markets as opposed to state intervention.

Privatisation moves firms from public to private ownership and is justified by both the Conservative government and supporters of privatisation largely in terms of the argument that private ownership and competition go together while public ownership is instead associated with tendencies towards monopoly and government protection through subsidy. Therefore, in the minds of City supporters of privatisation the change in mode of ownership from public to private is also a move from monopoly and subsidy to markets and competition. Consequently, for interviewees the questions about privatisation are in effect questions about markets. Similarly, the topic of progressive income taxation taps the interviewees' views of markets because individuals working in the City view progressive income taxation largely as a more or less justified (or unjustified) interference with the distributional outcomes of market processes. Finally, the issue of government policy on unemployment raises the problem in the

20

minds of interviewees as to whether the government should rely on market processes to reduce unemployment to acceptable levels rather than on Keynesian policies involving massive programmes of public spending.

Views about privatisation were elicited by asking questions about the privatisation of BT (British Telecom), which had recently taken place, and the overall privatisation policy of the government. The questions were as follows. First, 'What was your attitude to the privatisation of BT (British Telecom)? Were you: in favour, opposed or somewhere in between?'. Interviewees were then asked what grounds in their view there were for and against the sell-off. This and the similar follow-up question on the overall privatisation policy: 'What is your attitude to the overall privatisation policy? Are you: in favour, opposed or somewhere in between?', provide valuable data about how the interviewees think about the relationship between the market and the state. Interviewees were then asked what grounds in their view there were for and against the overall privatisation policy.

On progressive income taxation, interviewees were asked, 'Do you support or oppose a progressive income tax or do you have some other opinion?'.[2] The interviewee was then asked which grounds for and against a progressive income tax carried weight for him or her. The questions about progressive income tax, as argued earlier, were a useful indicator of an interviewee's general view of the legitimacy of state 'interference' in the distributional outcomes of market processes. The follow-up questions provided evidence about the extent to which the interviewee approved or disapproved of egalitarian aims. Since egalitarian views tend to conflict with pro-market views (chapter 5 below), any comments about equality and inequality made by the interviewee are additional evidence about an individual's views about the role of markets.

Finally, in the later interviews, the interviewee was asked about the government's policy on reducing unemployment. Halfway through the fieldwork, concern about unemployment appeared to be growing in Britain and even many government supporters were anxious about what they saw as an over-reliance upon market forces.[3] The question asked in interviews deliberately posed the issue in terms of government responsibility to reduce unemployment in order to tap the interviewee's view on the proper relationship of state and market. The interviewee was asked, 'Is the government doing enough about unemployment?'. The interviewee was then asked to explain why she or he held the view expressed. The follow-up question provided the researcher with valuable clarification of the initial answer.

The data in this chapter support the argument introduced in chapter 1 that City people tend to generalise from their experience of financial markets to all economic sectors. Whether confronting questions about privatisation, progressive income tax or unemployment policy, interviewees with few exceptions assume that all markets are like financial markets and that the market mechanism with little or no state intervention is adequate for solving all economic problems.

The organisation of the rest of the chapter is as follows. Sections 2, 3 and 4 present and analyse data about the opinions of interviewees on privatisation, progressive income tax and unemployment policy. Section 5 compares interviewees' opinions on the above topics to those of the wider population.

2   PRIVATISATION

(a) Opinions about privatisation

Ninety-five people were asked whether they had favoured, opposed or taken an intermediate position on the privatisation of British Telecom (BT); 96 people were questioned about their opinion of the Conservative government's overall privatisation programme: did they favour or oppose it or take an intermediate position? The responses are summarised in Table 2.1.

TABLE 2.1   *Opinions about privatisation*

| | Percentage expressing each opinion | |
| | ISSUE | |
Opinion expressed	Privatisation of British Telecom	Privatisation Policy
Favours	81%	75%
Mixed view	6%	17%
Opposes	13%	7%
Other	0%	2%
No. of individuals asked about issue	95	96

Table 2.1 is evidence of the strong pro-market views of interviewees. The overwhelming majority support both the privatisation of BT and the overall privatisation programme.

In between the supporters and opponents of privatisation stand those with 'mixed views'. On the BT sale, individuals coded 'Mixed view' were neither unequivocal supporters nor opponents: they referred to advantages and disadvantages of the stock market launch. On the overall programme, individuals classified as 'Mixed view' were in favour of certain privatisations and opposed others and also expressed arguments for and against the privatisation programme. A higher proportion were able to come to a definite decision about the sell-off of BT – which had, incidentally, been sold more aggressively than any other firm privatised to that time – than about the general programme. Thus, only 6 per cent were coded 'Mixed view' about BT while 17 per cent were so coded on the overall programme.

Opponents of both the BT sell-off and the overall policy constituted small minorities. In order to calculate more precisely the extent to which interviewees were critical of privatisation and supportive of public ownership or the mixed economy, the answers of all interviewees to the question about the overall privatisation programme were carefully examined (see also the analysis of Table 2.5). Those who claimed to oppose the overall policy number seven. Of these seven, only five reject the privatisation policy totally or virtually totally. The remaining two individuals asserted that they opposed a systematic privatisation policy but indicated that they favoured sales of firms which they did not regard as essential parts of the public sector (for example, Amersham International or Cable and Wireless which had been privatised before BT). None of the five outright opponents of privatisation expressed any wide-ranging criticism of the market: three merely expressed admiration for what they perceived as the achievements of public ownership.

In addition to the seven individuals who claimed to oppose the overall policy, six other individuals did not oppose all privatisation but rejected most of the programme; a further 12 interviewees expressed serious reservations about parts but strongly supported other parts of the privatisation programme; finally, two expressed mixed feelings about the BT sale but otherwise supported the policy. In total 23 (I exclude the last two mentioned) individuals out of 97 who were asked one or other privatisation question expressed appreciable reservations about or opposed the privatisation programme. These individuals are the only interviewees with any serious doubts about privatisation. Indeed, if the opinions of interviewees about privatisation are a reliable guide to City opinion, the debate that takes place in the City about this aspect of the relationship between state intervention and the market concerns the extent and pace of privatisation rather than whether privatisation should take place at all.

(b) Grounds for and against privatisation

Few readers will be surprised by figures showing strongly favourable attitudes to privatisation among City people. It is of greater interest to examine the considerations which carry weight in the minds of interviewees when they confront the issues of the privatisation of BT and the privatisation programme. After each individual was asked for an opinion of the BT sell-off, he or she was asked to summarise the advantages and disadvantages of the BT sale. A similar question was asked after an opinion had been expressed about the overall privatisation programme. In Tables 2.2 to 2.5 and in the accompanying analysis, individual items mentioned by interviewees when asked to review the advantages and disadvantages of privatisation are referred to as 'grounds' for or against privatisation.

Before reviewing the grounds advanced both for and against privatisation, the distinction used below between 'economic' and 'political' grounds requires clarification. The adjective 'economic' has been attached to arguments about the performance of firms; the term 'political' refers to more general or abstract reasons (for example, a concern with the assets of the community or a preference for a particular kind of economic system). It should not be assumed that the distinction implies that 'economic' arguments are objective while 'political' ones are wholly subjective. The terms are used merely to distinguish between the kind of grounds to which appeal was made.

When asked for the advantages and disadvantages of privatisation, some individuals mentioned more than one ground for and/or more than one ground against privatisation whilst others advanced no reasons for and/or against. Tables 2.2 to 2.5 refer to the number of mentions of each ground and the total

TABLE 2.2   *Grounds for privatisation of BT*

Ground advanced for sale of BT	No. of mentions of each reason among:			
	all asked question	supporters of privatisation of BT	those with mixed views about privatising BT	opponents of privatisation of BT
Efficiency	47	43	4	0
Improved service	18	17	1	0
Employee motivation	10	10	0	0
Competition increases	13	10	3	0
Rigours of stock market a good discipline	5	3	2	0
Accountable to share holders	9	9	0	0
Good for City	5	5	0	0
'Political'	16	16	0	0
No reason not to	3	3	0	0
Other	1	1	0	0
Total reasons in support	124	113	10	0
Total individuals in each group	95	77	6	12

number of grounds cited. The number of individuals involved is indicated in the last line of each table.

Grounds advanced for (Tables 2.2 and 2.3) and against (Tables 2.4 and 2.5) privatisation are examined in turn.

(i) Grounds for Privatisation

Examination of Tables 2.2 and 2.3 shows that the small minority who opposed the sale of BT did not mention (Table 2.2) one

TABLE 2.3   *Grounds for the overall privatisation programme*

Ground advanced in favour of policy	No. of mentions of each reason among:			
	all asked question	supporters of privatisation	those with mixed views	opponents of privatisation
Efficiency	48	36	11	0
Improved service	6	6	0	0
Employee motivation	9	9	0	0
Competition increases	11	9	2	0
Rigours of stock market a good discipline	5	2	2	1
Accountable to share holders	7	7	0	0
Good for City	3	2	1	0
'Political'	35	35	0	0
No reason not to	4	4	0	0
Other	1	1	0	0
Total reasons in support	129	111	14	1
Total individuals in each group	96*	71	46	7

*Total includes two individuals not included in any of the columns to the right: one expressed no opinion about privatisation (merely mentioning efficiency as a ground); the other asserted that ownership is irrelevant (only efficiency matters).

ground in favour of privatisation – they clearly saw no virtue whatsoever in the stock market launch. The opponents of the overall programme managed between them to provide (Table 2.3) one ground in support of the policy.

Among supporters of the BT sale the overwhelming majority of grounds in favour of privatisation (Table 2.2) had to do with how privatisation would improve the business performance of BT. In other words supporters relied on 'economic' rather than 'political' arguments for privatisation. Ninety-two (81 per cent) out of 113 grounds advanced by supporters of the BT launch referred to improved performance: improved efficiency, improved service, higher employee motivation, the benefits of more competition, the beneficial effects on a firm of continuous stock market scrutiny and the similar advantages of accountability to shareholders.

'Political' grounds for privatisation of BT advanced by supporters constitute only 14 per cent of all grounds advanced by this group. The arguments coded 'political' include: references to the connection between privatisation and greater individual freedom; assertions that privatisation of BT would decrease bureaucracy in our society; assertions that the state should not run industries; one claim that the launch is part of a worldwide 'attempt to create more freedom'; and, finally, one individual supported the BT sale because 'the left-wing' opposed it. Another notable ground in favour of the BT privatisation included increased business for City firms[4] (coded 'Good for City'). In addition to the positive reasons in favour of the BT sale, three people stated categorically that there was no reason not to privatise: I have coded this as a reason to privatise.

With respect to the overall privatisation programme, supporters again rely mainly (Table 2.3) on 'economic' grounds: 69 (62 per cent) out of 111 grounds in favour. However, improved business performance was less frequently asserted as a ground in favour of the overall programme than for the BT sale – respectively 62 per cent as compared to 81 per cent of all grounds. The 62 per cent of grounds termed 'economic' include references to greater efficiency, improved service, increased employee motivation, the benefits of more competition, the virtues of stock market scrutiny and accountability to shareholders.

Correspondingly, 'political' grounds assumed greater significance when the general issue of privatisation – the overall programme – was discussed: 35 (32 per cent) out of 111 grounds advanced in favour of the overall policy as compared with only 16 out of 113 (14 per cent) of the grounds advanced for supporting the BT launch. 'Political' grounds in favour of the overall policy include: the benefits of wider share ownership;[5] assertions that the state should not run industries; the connection between privatisation and individualism; and the decrease in bureaucracy.

Individuals with 'mixed views' on the BT sale advanced (Table 2.2) only 'economic' grounds in favour (expectations of improved business performance). No 'political' grounds were mentioned in favour of privatisation by this group: none fitted into the 'Doctrinal' category. On the overall programme, individuals with 'mixed views' mentioned (Table 2.3) 14 grounds in favour of the programme: 13 (93 per cent) were to do with business performance and one mention was made of the boost to City business (coded 'Good for City'). Thus, this group shows no evidence of any 'political' commitment in favour of privatisation.

(ii) Grounds against Privatisation

Data on the grounds advanced against the privatisation of BT and the overall privatisation programme are summarised in Tables 2.4 and 2.5 respectively.

TABLE 2.4   *Grounds against privatisation of BT*

| Ground against BT sell-off | Number of mentions of each reason among: | | | |
	all asked question	supporters of BT sell-off	those with mixed views	opponents of BT sell-off
Monopolies should be state-owned	9	4	2	3
State asset	9	2	1	6
Offer price too low	11	6	1	4
Government case doctrinaire	8	0	2	6
No reason to privatise	4	0	0	4
Other	10	5	2	3
Total reasons to oppose	51	17	8	26
Total individuals in each group	95	77	6	12

The following points emerge from a study of Tables 2.4 and 2.5. The opponents of privatisation advanced (Table 2.4) a mixture of 'economic' and 'political' grounds against the BT sale, neither type of ground against being preponderant. Thus, seven out of 26 grounds mentioned were broadly (although not wholly) 'economic' arguments. This total of seven includes the codings 'Monopolies should be state-owned' and 'Offer price too low'. In addition, six mentions were made of BT being a state asset and this is partly an 'economic' argument (assets generate income) and partly a 'political' argument (one ought not to sell off public/communal assets). The arguments coded 'Government is doctrinaire' refer to criticisms of the government's belief that

TABLE 2.5   *Grounds against privatisation programme*

Ground advanced in favour of policy	Number of mentions of each reason among:			
	all asked question	supporters of privatisation	those with mixed views	opponents of privatisation
Monopolies should be state-owned	3	2	1	0
State assets	6	1	2	3
Government is doctrinaire	13	3	6	4
Pro-mixed economy	7	0	4	3
Pro-public ownership	4	0	3	1
No reason to privatise	3	0	0	3
Other	3	2	1	0
Total grounds against	39	8	17	14
Total individuals in each group	96*	71	16	7

*Total includes two individuals not included in any of the columns to the right: one expressed no opinion about privatisation (merely mentioning efficiency as a ground): the other asserted that ownership is irrelevant (only efficiency matters).

private firms are necessarily better performers than state-owned ones. Such grounds against (six mentions) the BT sale are treated as 'political' grounds. Finally, four mentions were explicitly made of there being no reasons whatsoever to privatise BT.

On the overall privatisation programme, grounds against advanced by opponents (Table 2.5) were overwhelmingly 'political'. The opponents did not even mention the 'economic' ground against coded 'Monopolies should be state owned'. Three individuals used the argument that state assets should not be sold which is partly an 'economic' and partly a 'political' ground against. All other specific grounds against were 'political': 'Government is doctrinaire'; 'Pro-mixed economy' (the individual favours a mixed economy); 'Pro-public ownership' (the individual favours public ownership for certain firms or industries). The significance of the neglect of 'economic' arguments by opponents of the privatisation programme will be explored below.

It is notable that supporters of both the BT sell-off and the overall programme mentioned relatively few grounds against privatisation: 77 supporters of the BT sale mentioned 17 grounds against and 71 supporters of the overall programme mentioned only eight grounds against. Supporters of the BT sell-off were more likely to mention (Table 2.4) 'economic' than 'political' grounds against the sell-off, the former constituting ten (59 per cent) out of the 17 reasons advanced against. Economic arguments are coded 'Monopolies should be state-owned' and 'Issue price too low'. In addition, as previously argued, an element of the 'State asset' argument (two mentions) is economic. None of the supporters of the BT sale actually stated that the government case was 'doctrinaire', although two of the responses coded 'Other' came close to this: the government is going a bit too fast; no reason why a privatised BT should be more efficient.

No supporter of the overall programme mentioned (Table 2.5) a positive commitment to a 'mixed economy', although the three mentions of the government being doctrinaire are implicit statements of a belief that the privately-owned joint-stock company is not always the most appropriate solution.

Other arguments against were 'economic', 'Monopolies should be state-owned', or a mixture of political and economic in the case of the coding 'State assets' and one of the grounds coded 'Other'.

On the BT sell-off individuals with 'mixed views' advanced

(Table 2.4) both 'political' and 'economic' grounds against although, taking account of the 'Other' category, economic objections were rather more common. On the overall privatisation programme those with 'mixed views' (like the opponents) were more likely to advance (Table 2.5) 'political' grounds against than was the case on the BT sale, 'political' grounds against the programme constitute 13 (76 per cent) of 17 grounds mentioned. Only one ground against was clearly 'economic' although, of course, grounds coded 'State assets' are partly 'economic' and partly 'political'.

(c) Summary and critical examination of opinions about privatisation

Table 2.1 shows the overwhelming support amongst interviewees for the privatisation of BT and the overall privatisation programme.

Analysis of grounds for the BT sale shows the following. First, supporters relied mainly on 'economic' grounds referring to improved business performance rather than on 'political' grounds, although some mention was made of the latter. Second, those with 'mixed views' about the BT sale relied exclusively on economic arguments. Third, opponents of the BT sale were unable to see any arguments at all in favour.

When the sample was asked about the overall privatisation programme, supporters were far more likely to present 'political' grounds in favour than was the case when the specific BT sell-off was discussed. However, supporters of the overall policy still attached greater weight to 'economic' than 'political' arguments. Those with 'mixed views' mentioned (as was the case with the BT sale) only 'economic' grounds in favour of the overall programme. Opponents of the programme advanced between them only one mention of a ground for privatisation: a reference to the stock market providing a good discipline for firms.

What is striking about the grounds for privatisation presented by supporters is the confidence with which these were deployed. As mentioned in chapter 1, pro-market views go virtually unchallenged in the ideologically closed world of the City. Interviewees are probably no different from those working outside the City in that they often appear unaware of strong counter-arguments to their views. What makes the City different from most occupational worlds is the relative ideological homogeneity of the City (see chapter 5). It is this homogeneity which makes it so easy to ignore other approaches to privatisation. Weak and unsystematic arguments thrive in such environments.

For example, one interviewee's anecdotal 'argument' for privatisation illustrates the generally unsystematic and uncritical approach to the privatisation issue. As evidence for the benefits of privatisation, he mentioned that recently the post-privatisation BT engineer turned up to repair his telephone more quickly than would have been the case pre-privatisation.

Similarly, and more importantly, City supporters of privatisation use the argument of greater 'competition' to justify privatisation without (except very occasionally) even hinting at the complexity of the concept of 'competition'.

In chapter 1, it was argued that City people generalise their experience of competition in financial markets to all markets and this represents an unreflective use of the concept. Grounds for privatisation presented by its supporters display a similarly unreflective application of the concept of 'competition'. Grounds for privatisation presented by supporters again and again included reference to the alleged necessarily greater competitiveness of privately-owned firms. Indeed, all the 'economic' grounds in Tables 2.2 and 2.3 (greater 'Efficiency', 'Improved service' to customers, better 'Employee motivation', 'Competition increases', 'Rigours of stock market a good discipline', 'Accountable to shareholders') are bound up with the idea of the necessarily greater competitiveness of privately-owned firms.

Admittedly, interviews did not allow individuals much time to develop arguments but they did allow time for at least some to hint at the complexity of the matters discussed. For example, few supporters of the privatisation programme remarked (Table 2.5) on the fact that privatising a monopoly does not necessarily generate much competition – even they assumed that a private monopoly is always preferable. Despite the sweeping claims about the association between increased competition and privatisation, only one supporter of privatisation remarked on the fact that even state-owned monopolies have to compete (British Rail with road and air transport; the then state-owned British Gas with the Electricity Boards). For virtually all supporters of privatisation 'competition' is no more than an unexamined concept which is used to justify a favoured political conclusion: privatisation.

Indeed, taking account of all interviewees, only one (a young merchant banker), who had 'mixed views' on the BT sale and the overall programme, demonstrated any deep understanding of the complexity of the issues surrounding the relationship between privatisation and greater competitiveness. She discussed in some detail the manner in which what she referred to as the government's 'doctrinaire' commitment to privatisation as always the best solution leads them to ignore possibilities of genuinely increasing competition in an industry. She referred to the way the government favoured British Airways as against British Caledonian in route allocations to push up the offer price of British Airways shares whenever British Airways should be privatised. She clearly understood that competition and privatisation are different and not always compatible goals. Her arguments are similar to those of Vickers and Yarrow who suggest that, if the government is serious about wishing to increase competition and improve the service to consumers, they ought to concentrate on this aim rather than assuming that privatisation automatically achieves the result they claim to desire.[6]

The explanation for the fact that only a minority of supporters of privatisation have made a real effort to grapple with the complex arguments involved is that the culture of the City makes genuine debate about the relationship between state and market or about the respective virtues of private versus communal ownership difficult if not impossible for most individuals. Serious debate about such matters is virtually taboo: the virtues of privatisation are an article of faith in the City.

Reasons not to privatise were far less often mentioned because the overwhelming majority of individuals in the sample favoured privatisation. Grounds advanced against privatisation dramatise the weak support for public ownership of particular industries and for the principle of a 'mixed' economy, even one in which the 'mix' has moved in favour of the private ownership element. None of the 71 supporters of the overall privatisation programme made an explicit mention of positive attitudes to either. On the other hand, the 23 individuals who were either opponents of or held 'mixed views' on the overall programme managed between them to produce 11 mentions of pro-public ownership or pro-mixed economy grounds against the programme (Table 2.5). None of these 23 interviewees wished to extend public ownership: they wished to maintain a public sector of some kind, albeit often a reduced one.

Supporters of privatisation did sometimes mention grounds against the BT sale and the overall policy. On BT, the arguments against presented by supporters were to do with the 'low' issue price, the sale of a 'state asset' and the danger of private monopolies; no one spoke in favour of public ownership as a principle for a large national, basic industry. On the overall policy, the 71 supporters presented eight mentions of grounds against whilst mentioning 111 grounds in favour: this is an indication of the strength of their support for the programme.

Individuals with 'mixed views' on privatisation were, not surprisingly, able to think pretty equally both of arguments against and in favour of the BT sale and the overall policy. Unlike the supporters of privatisation, some explicitly spoke in favour of the 'mixed economy' and of a degree of public ownership rather than relying purely on arguments about the likely results on the performance of firms.

Finally, opponents of the BT sale mentioned no grounds in favour and opponents of the overall programme mentioned one between them. Opponents concentrated virtually all their attention on the grounds against and the grounds advanced tended not to be arguments about business performance although those concerned expressed scepticism about claims for the improved performance of privatised firms.

Effectively, opponents neglected 'economic' grounds against in favour of 'political' grounds such as a belief in a 'mixed economy' or the need for public ownership of certain industries. Other grounds against included criticisms of selling state (or communal) assets (this is a partly 'political' and partly 'economic' ground) and a concern that certain goods and services should always be available to those in need even if such people could not afford to buy them in the market. The only wholly 'economic' grounds against – that is, arguments about the performance of firms – which attracted the interest of this group appeared on the topic of the BT sale: these were references to the arguments against private monopolies and the issue price of BT being 'too low'. Both these 'economic' grounds against are respectable in the city. The neglect of 'economic' grounds against privatisation may be significant: the culture of the City is heavily based on the assumption that the business performance (return on capital employed) of privately-owned firms (that is, as opposed to those owned by the state or the community) is always superior and that the only valid grounds for communal/state ownership are social or political. Presumably, even strong City opponents of privatisation find it difficult to challenge this cultural assumption.

Despite the fact that opponents of privatisation advanced virtually no grounds in its favour, they had clearly been forced to consider arguments in favour because the environment in which they work is so favourable to privatisation and the market. The contrary is seldom true in the case of supporters of privatisation.

3 PROGRESSIVE INCOME TAX

This section analyses interviewees' views on progressive income tax.

(a) Support for and opposition to progressive income tax

Eighty-six interviewees were asked whether they favoured progressive income tax, opposed progressive income tax or had some other opinion. Table 2.6 summarises the answers.

Individuals coded 'Favours' expressed support for the system where rates rise in stages from 30 pence to 60 pence in the pound (the rates in force at the time of the fieldwork in 1985). Individuals coded as 'Favours weakly' supported the principle of some progression but criticised higher rates as excessive and/or 'unfair' and/or as being a disincentive to hard work; such individuals come very close at times to being in favour of a flat rate, that is, to being classified as 'Opposed'. Interviewees coded 'Opposed' flatly opposed the principle of progressive taxation.

TABLE 2.6   *Opinions about progressive income tax*

View of progressive income tax	Percentage in each category
Favours	56%
Favours weakly	23%
Opposes	16%
Inconsistent	1%
Incoherent	1%
Other	2%
Total asked question	87

There are two ways to look at these figures: (a) nearly four fifths (79 per cent) either accept ('Favours weakly') or positively support ('Favours') the present system; (b) nearly two fifths (39

TABLE 2.7   *Grounds for progressive income tax*

Ground in favour of PIT	Number of mentions of ground irrespective of opinion of PIT	Sample broken down by opinion of Progressive Income Tax (PIT)		
		Favours PIT	Favours PIT weakly	Opposes PIT
Pit is fair	36	29	7	0
Pragmatism: only way to raise sufficient money	17	11	3	1
Help the poor	10	6	3	1
Better off should pay more	2	2	0	0
More equal society favoured	7	5	2	0
There are no good arguments against PIT	4	4	0	0
Total mentions of grounds for PIT	76	57	15	2
Number of individuals who did not mention any grounds for PIT	24	6	7	11
Total individuals in each group	87*	49	20	14

*Columns to right only include those coded as supporting or opposing progressive income tax. The four excluded individuals were discussed above.

per cent) favour a reduction or elimination of even the degree of progression which still existed after 1979.

Two factors which may reduce City opposition to progressive income tax need emphasising. First, at the time of the interviews the income tax system in the United Kingdom was formally redistributive from higher to lower income groups. In practice higher rate taxpayers (especially those paying 50 pence or 60 pence in the pound) had many opportunities to reduce the proportion of income paid in income tax.[7] Furthermore the top rate of income tax had already been reduced sharply soon after the Conservatives won the 1979 general election and this meant that many interviewees regarded the existing bands relatively favourably (and the top rate has been reduced even further since the research was carried out).

Five individuals could not be classified as either supporters or opponents of progressive income tax (Table 2.6). Consideration of such individuals exemplifies the kind of problems confronted when analysing and coding political statements. First, a 'blue-button' (that is, trainee) jobber[8] coded 'Incoherent' made the following statements: progressive income tax is the only means to raise sufficient revenue because the poor cannot afford to pay as much as people earning more; the current tax rates are too high and reduce incentives; the 'middling' suffer most from the present income tax system because the rich hire accountants. Two individuals were coded 'Other' because they neither supported nor opposed progressive income tax. One[9] stated that he had no view about the legitimacy of progressive income tax: it was merely a means to raise revenue; if needed, it should be used and vice versa. The other[10] preferred an expenditure tax: the share of income actually spent would be taxed at progressive rates; this tax would be allied to a flat-rate income tax.

What grounds did interviewees, whatever their opinions of progressive income tax, advance for and against progressive income tax? Analysis of these grounds will help us to understand how interviewees perceive progressive income tax.

(b) Grounds for progressive income tax

Data on the grounds for progressive income tax advanced by interviewees are presented in Table 2.7.

Table 2.7 shows that by far the most common ground advanced for progressive income tax is that 'progressive income tax is fair': 59 per cent of those coded 'Favours' progressive income tax mentioned this as a ground in favour. Only 35 per cent of those coded 'Favours weakly' mentioned this as an argument for progressive income tax and, as one would expect, none of the opponents of progressive income tax did so. The second most frequent ground in favour of progressive income tax is 'Pragmatism', that is, the view that the only way to raise sufficient revenue is to tax higher incomes more heavily than lower incomes. This ground was more popular among supporters of progressive income tax than among those who favoured progressive income tax weakly or opposed it. The third most common ground for progressive income tax was to 'Help the poor': mention of this ground does not indicate an egalitarian preference; the notion here is that certain individuals cannot earn enough in the market and have to be supplied with the means to meet basic needs through the state social security system. Eight per cent of those asked the question favoured progressive income tax on the ground 'More equal society favoured' – this ground is distinct from 'Help the poor' in that a preference for greater equality involves a policy for the whole range of income (and wealth) rather than one which is merely concerned with the incomes of the very poorest.

Of those who expressed a desire for a more equal society, five had been coded 'Favours' progressive income tax but two individuals had been coded 'Favours weakly'. The latter two individuals merit examination because one would normally expect an egalitarian to be coded 'Favours' progressive income tax. First, a young jobber[11] was coded 'Favours weakly' because he claimed to favour progressive income tax on the grounds of fairness and greater equality but expressed concern about the disincentive effects of what he sees as excessive taxation of high incomes:

> It's a way of redistributing wealth. As long as it's not too severe, I suppose it is fair that higher earners do pay a greater proportion of those higher earnings into the system.

Second, a young merchant banker[12] was coded 'Favours weakly' because, although she claimed to support progressive income tax and said, in response to the question about arguments for progressive income tax: 'I'm a socialist at heart and so I essentially believe in the redistribution of wealth', she immediately proceeded to complain about the 'killing tax burdens' in the UK, which she sees as a disincentive to enterprise. It should be noted that both these interviewees appear to confuse income and wealth taxation.

Finally, four individuals coded 'Favours' stated that there were no good arguments against progressive income tax – this was coded as a ground for progressive income tax.

(c) Grounds against progressive income tax

Table 2.8 summarises the data on the grounds against progressive income tax mentioned by interviewees.

It is striking how few of the opponents of progressive income tax mention what is effectively an ethical ground against, namely that 'progressive income tax is unfair', which is mentioned by only three individuals coded 'Opposes'. The most popular objection to progressive income tax in all groups is that it undermines incentives (coded 'Need for incentives'): indeed, mention of incentives totalled 30 out of 46 grounds against. This is an 'economic' rather than a 'political' (or ethical) ground against progressive income tax and it conforms well to the pro-market views of the interviewees.

The 'Other' category in Table 2.8 is relatively large and merits analysis. In the group which 'Opposes' progressive income tax, the following comments were classified as 'Other':

(a) a flat-rate income tax would be a more efficient method to raise required revenue (interviewee did not clarify because time was short);

(b) most of the higher-paid have considerable influence over their own incomes and will respond to high rates of tax of their incomes by raising their pre-tax income – this will leave less over for the lower-paid and for investment to create jobs;

(c) rewards in the market reflect hard work and progressive income tax interferes with this relationship;

(d) everyone has an equal say in government and, therefore, everyone should pay the same (absolute not proportionate) amount of tax.

In the 'Favours' progressive income tax group, the remark classified 'Other' referred to a worry about the double-taxation of savings: savings are from post-tax income but later the income

TABLE 2.8   *Grounds against a progressive income tax*

Ground against PIT	Number of mentions of ground irrespective of opinion of PIT	Sample broken down by opinion of Progressive Income tax (PIT)		
		Favours PIT	Favours PIT weakly	Opposes PIT
PIT is unfair	5	0	1	3
Need for incentives	30	11	10	8
No good grounds for PIT	1	0	0	1
Other	10	1	1	4
Number of mentions of grounds against PIT	46	12	12	16
Number of individuals who did not mention any grounds against PIT	50	38	8	1
Total individuals in each group	87*	49	20	14

*Columns to right include only those coded as supporting or opposing progressive income tax. The four excluded individuals were discussed above.

they generate will be taxed. This person preferred an expenditure tax under which only the portion of income spent would be taxed. In the 'Favours weakly' group the statement categorised 'Other' is that heavily taxed high earnings will encourage the most able to emigrate and this will produce a loss of jobs since industry depends on their leadership.

One individual stated there were 'No good grounds for progressive income tax': this was coded as a ground against progressive income tax.

(d) Opinions about progressive income tax: summary and conclusions

Table 2.6 shows majority support amongst the 86 interviewees questioned about income tax, for the progressive income tax system existing at the time of the fieldwork. Fifty-six per cent were firm supporters of progressive income tax; 23 per cent believed that the progression of the system should be weakened further by, for example, cutting the top rate to 45 per cent or 50 per cent. Only 16 per cent, however, stated that they opposed progressive income tax outright: a rather small group considering the reputation of the City. It is likely that the existence of many tax avoidance schemes for the highly paid and wealthy does lessen explicit opposition to formally progressive income taxation.

The most frequent grounds advanced in favour of progressive income tax were fairness and pragmatism. By 'pragmatism', is meant the argument that progressive income tax is the only way to raise the necessary revenue since the poorer cannot pay as high a proportion in income tax as other better off individuals. Few people mentioned support for progressive income tax on the basis of a desire for greater equality and in two out of seven cases this was qualified seriously. By far the most frequently articulated ground against progressive income tax is that it denies incentives to the hardworking and enterprising.

Only the 'Opposes' progressive income tax group (16 per cent) can be said to hold pure pro-market views about income tax. The 'Favours weakly' group (22 per cent) have some doubts about the principle of progressive income tax and/or wish to reduce the progressiveness of the system but they cannot be considered to hold pure pro-market views albeit that their views tend in this direction.

What is interesting is that over half (56 per cent) were coded 'Favours' progressive income tax. Most of these would support the pro-market privatisation policy but appear to dilute their pro-market views in respect of progressive income tax. This statement of support for progressive income tax probably reflects, first, the enormous legitimacy in the United Kingdom of some degree of progression in the income tax system and, second, their awareness of the many means to reduce the impact of the formal progressiveness of the system.

4   GOVERNMENT POLICY AND UNEMPLOYMENT

When the fieldwork was being carried out, unemployment was above three million, even according to widely disputed government figures.[13] Interviewees were asked, 'Is the government doing enough about unemployment?' and were requested to explain the grounds for their view. The aim of the question was to discover whether the interviewees favoured a wholly market-based strategy or would advocate or accept a higher level of state intervention, especially increased state spending, as a means to reduce unemployment. This question was adopted in the middle of the fieldwork period and was asked in 47 interviews only. Interviewees' opinions are summarised in Table 2.9.

TABLE 2.9   *Is the government doing enough about unemployment?*

Reply	Percentage in category
Government is doing enough	38%
Government is not doing enough	47%
Undecided/Inconsistent	15%
Number of individuals asked about unemployment	47

(a) Views on unemployment

Nearly a half (47 per cent) of those questioned were unhappy in one way or another with the government's policy and achievements up to the Spring or early Summer of 1985. Critics usually but by no means always wanted the government to reduce their reliance on a pure market-based strategy but this seldom involved anything like a whole-hearted Keynesian interventionist strategy.

It should be noted that 71 (84 per cent) of the 86 interviewees who disclosed how they voted in the General Election of 1983 stated that they had voted Conservative. Government critics included: 17 Conservative voters; one Labour voter; three Alliance voters; one non-voter who had been unable to decide between the Conservatives and the Alliance; one individual who refused to say how he had voted. Thus, government critics were not predominantly non-Conservatives: indeed, one of the Alliance supporters was a former Conservative who had switched largely because of unemployment. Presumably, this unease about unemployment reflected the growing anxiety in the country at large, even amongst Conservatives, remarked upon earlier in the chapter.

However, note that 38 per cent still wholly supported the government's market-based economic strategy which assigns priority to inflation and the control of public spending rather than unemployment.

(b) What should the Government do about unemployment?

After interviewees had given an opinion about whether the government was doing enough about unemployment, they were asked what, if anything, more should or could the government do? Answers effectively took the form of remarks about unemployment policy and the unemployed. Data are presented in Table 2.10.

Fourteen interviewees stated that the government should 'Increase state spending': ten of these were individuals dissatisfied with government policy. However, only a handful of these individuals wished for a complete break with the government's policy. In addition, one individual (remark coded 'Other' in Table 2.10) stated that the market-based strategy had failed and he would support a 'complete reversal': he became irritable when he was asked for clarification. His remark was fascinating because he was in other respects strongly pro-market: he supported the privatisation of all industries owned by the state and opposed progressive income tax.

Remarks which are explicitly favourable to market-based solutions to high unemployment rather than interventionist policies are included in the top seven codings: the importance of 'Self-help', state should 'Assist entrepreneurs', we need to 'Increase wage/labour flexibility', the government policy is adequate and we should 'Wait for policy to take effect', 'Welfare state blamed' (people now rely on handouts, and so forth),[14] 'Unemployed criticised' for laziness or lack of initiative, unemployed should 'Work for benefits'. The seven codings just mentioned constitute 18 remarks and to these can be added two

TABLE 2.10 *Remarks about unemployment*

Remark made	All asked question irrespective of answer	Respondents broken down by opinion of government policy		
		Doing enough	Not doing enough	Undecided/ Inconsistent
Self-help	2	0	2	0
Assist en-trepreneurs	5	2	2	1
Increase wage/Labour flexibility	2	0	2	0
Wait for policy to take effect	3	3	0	0
Welfare state blamed	3	3	0	0
Unemployed criticised	2	1	1	0
Work for benefits	1	1	0	0
Increase state spending	14	2	10	2
Figures exaggerate	2	1	1	0
PR problem	3	1	2	0
Inevitable	4	2	0	2
Priority of inflation	3	2	0	1
Other	19	3	13	3
Number in each group	47	18	22	7

remarks coded 'Other' which express a market-based approach to the problem. The remarks concerned were: praise for the government's Youth Training Scheme together with a claim that people do get jobs afterwards – the interviewee knew two individuals who had; a statement that the government could not create 'real' jobs. Altogether these remarks constitute 20 (33 per cent) out of a total 61 remarks. This rises to 23 (38 per cent) if one includes the defence of the government's policy coded 'Priority of inflation' over unemployment. In addition, remarks coded 'Figures exaggerate' the true extent of the problem, the government policy faced a 'PR problem' were all really defences of the government's market-based policy. If we add these remarks, 31 (51 per cent) of the remarks were defences of the market-based policy at a time when confidence in the policy was at a very low point. Note that those who approve of government policy do not have a monopoly of such remarks although they utter them less frequently. Overall these figures indicate how pro-market the interviewees were even on a topic where market-based solutions were under exceptionally heavy attack from virtually all quarters.

The 'Other' category is large and diverse. Of particular interest are the following:

(a) a claim that the government could not find the money to increase state expenditure;

(b) the view, expressed by two individuals, that there is a need to re-educate people so that unemployment is no longer seen in itself as a deprivation (one of these advocated egalitarian measures to redistribute income and wealth);

(c) an assertion by a male merchant banker that, in the 1970s, many women were unemployed; often this unemployment was hidden because, frequently, women did not qualify for unemployment benefit; unemployment among women had not been noticed – unemployment only came to be perceived as a problem when men began to suffer badly;

(d) a jobber's concern about the 'degrading' effect of unemployment; he favoured more action by the government without knowing what they might do;

(e) three remarks advocating an earlier age of retirement and/or work-sharing.

(c) Government and unemployment: summary

First, nearly half (47 per cent) believed that the government was not doing enough about unemployment. However, 38 per cent of interviewees wholly supported the government's market-based strategy even at a point of particularly low confidence in the strategy. Second, the most frequent remark about what the government ought to do was that it should increase state spending. However, the majority of remarks (51 per cent) expressed clear pro-market sentiments in relation to unemployment policy.

5   INTERVIEWEES' OPINIONS AND BRITISH PUBLIC OPINION

Are interviewees' views on privatisation, income taxation and unemployment policy out of line with those prevailing within the wider population at roughly the same time? This section summarises some relevant data. Comparative data used below have been collected in the 1980s and this means that we are comparing interviewees' opinions to those of the wider population at roughly the same time.

(a) Privatisation

Table 2.1 shows that 75 per cent of interviewees support the government's policy that virtually all state-owned firms should be privatised. Eighty-one per cent supported the sale of BT (British Telecom). The opinions of those outside the City appear to be very different.

Heath, Jowell and Curtice[15] collected interview data from 3955 electors in 1983. In their analysis of class structure they identify the 'salariat' which consists of managers, administrators, professionals and other white collar workers other than routine white-collar workers.[16] Interviewees in the present study would fit this classification. Heath found[17] that 52 per cent of the salariat favoured privatisation as against 75 per cent of interviewees examined here. All other classes except the 'petty bourgeoisie' (farmers, small proprietors and own-account manual workers)[18] are less favourable to privatisation than the salariat: 66 per cent of this class favour privatisation. Heath, Jowell and Curtice[19] report that overall 42 per cent of respondents favoured privatisation while 40 per cent preferred no change and 18 per cent wanted further nationalisation.

K. Young[20] analysed data collected in 1984 and states that:

> Although it was the case that relatively few respondents wished to see increases in the extent of state ownership, the support for reductions (more 'privatization') was also fairly modest, at 36% overall, with slightly stronger support among men than women.

Young's data also show[21] that 50 per cent of individuals classified in Registrar General Social Classes 1 (Professional) and 11

(Intermediate Non-manual) wish to see less state ownership as compared to 75 per cent of interviewees in the present study who support the privatisation programme.

In an article in an earlier volume of the *British Social Attitudes* series[22] based upon data collected in 1983, Harrison shows that 68 per cent of respondents classified as having Conservative Party identification want less state ownership and these figures are much closer to interviewees' views although it must be emphasised that in addition to the 75 per cent of interviewees who support the privatisation programme, 17 per cent have 'Mixed views' and this involves support for some privatisation.

NOP Market Research Ltd. carried out a survey for the Trades Union Congress in October 1986.[23] Two years after the sale of BT, 53 per cent of respondents stated that BT should be publicly rather than privately owned while 37 per cent took the opposing view. In the case of electricity, gas and water the differences between the interviewees and the sample were also striking. Seventy-one per cent favoured public and 21 per cent favoured private ownership. In the cases of coal, rail and steel, 56 per cent favoured public and 33 per cent private ownership. In the cases of defence factories and Royal Naval Dockyards, 71 per cent favoured public and 15 per cent private ownership. In the case of the British Airports Authority, 49 per cent favoured public and 34 per cent private ownership. Finally in the case of local bus services, 55 per cent favoured public and 37 per cent private ownership. Overall, in the case of each industry about which NOP's respondents were questioned, public ownership was preferred sometimes by enormous margins.

It is clear from a consideration of the comparative data presented above that present interviewees are exceptionally pro-market by British standards as indicated by their views on privatisation.

(b) Progressive Income Taxation

Data discussed below sometimes lumps together income and wealth redistribution while the question asked in this study was only about income taxation. However, the comparative data analysed below allows of some conclusions about the typicality or otherwise of interviewees' opinions of progressive income taxation.

Anthony Harrison, in the article to which reference has already been made,[24] concludes after examining data collected in 1983 that:

> By more than a three to one majority the public thinks that the gap between high and low incomes is too large. . . . even among those in Social Class 1/11 . . . over half think that the gap is too large.

M. Mann[25] examined data collected in 1985 at roughly the same time as the data for the present study. He concludes with respect to British attitudes to income and wealth inequality that:

> By a ratio of 2:1 the sample felt that income and wealth in Britain should be redistributed towards ordinary working people. However, Conservatives disagreed markedly, and those in Social Classes 1 and 11 disagreed more than they agreed (41 per cent to 32 per cent). Should the government be involved in redistribution? We asked this in two slightly different ways. Sixty-nine per cent thought the government had a responsibility to reduce income differences between rich and poor, and only 24 per cent disagreed. Once again, however, Conservatives were more ambivalent. When we changed the wording from 'between rich and poor' to 'between those with high and those with low incomes', the proportion agreeing dropped to 52 per cent. Among Conservatives alone a majority disagreed, but among those in Social Classes 1 and 11 only a bare majority agreed.

This quotation shows strong support in the general population for redistributionary government policy, majority support in Social Classes 1 and 11 and further study of the article[26] suggests that the Conservative majority opposed to such redistribution is on the small side.

Finally, P. Taylor-Gooby[27] concludes from an examination of data collected in 1986 that although support for egalitarian measures is a 'remote' prospect, 77 per cent of respondents believe that those with higher incomes should pay a much larger proportion in taxes compared with those on lower incomes. Seventy-two per cent believe that the government definitely or probably should reduce income differences between rich and poor. However, as the questions are brought closer to home only 59 per cent agree strongly or agree that the government should reduce income differences between those on high and those on low incomes and only 43 per cent support redistribution from the better off to the less well off while 30 per cent disagree or disagree strongly.

How do the figures compare to the views of the present interviewees? Table 2.6 shows that 39 per cent of interviewees oppose or wish to dilute the present system of progressive income taxation. Table 2.7 indicates that only seven interviewees (8 per cent) out of 87 favour greater equality of income while ten interviewees (11 per cent) justify progressive income tax on the grounds that the poor should be helped and two others (2 per cent) state that the better off should pay more. Altogether 22 per cent of interviewees favour some redistribution, although this is usually only to the poorest.

Overall, although British opinion is by no means egalitarian, interviewees seem to be much less so than the general population on the issue of redistribution of income through the taxation system.

(c) Unemployment Policy

Mann[28] in the article referred to above states that:

> About two-thirds of our sample agreed that it was the government's responsibility to provide a job for everyone who wants one, and only 26% disagreed – a clear rejection of the government's present strategy of leaving employment largely to market forces.

The respondents showed enormous support of between 80 per cent and over 90 per cent for various policies: government financed projects to create new jobs and help to firms developing new products and technology. On support for declining industries to protect jobs 49 per cent supported the idea as against 29 per cent against. Heath, Jowell and Curtice report[29] that Conservative voters in the 1983 General Election showed 53 per cent support for the view that the government should create jobs while 35 per cent disagreed.

What does the above data suggest about the typicality of the opinions of interviewees in the present study on the issue of government responsibility for decreasing unemployment? Table 2.9 shows that 47 per cent of interviewees thought that the government in mid-1985 was not doing enough about unemployment and 38 per cent thought they were. It must be emphasised that the individuals unhappy with government policy were only in favour of Keynesian solutions in a handful of cases. These figures for the interviewees are very different from those reported by Mann for a sample representative of the general adult population but close to those for Conservative voters described by Heath, Jowell and Curtice. Interviewees, in other words, were more pro-market on unemployment policy than the general public in Britain at around the same time.

6 SUMMARY

The conclusions of this chapter are as follows. Interviewees support the privatisation programme by an enormous margin. The large majority accept or positively support the system of mild progressive income taxation in existence in 1985 but with many qualifications. On unemployment, almost half of interviewees were unhappy with the government's market-based strategy but the majority of remarks made by interviewees when asked to explain the grounds for their view expressed pro-market sentiments rather than Keynesian ones.

Comparison of the views just reported demonstrates that on privatisation and unemployment the interviewees are seriously out of line with general British attitudes. On income taxation and inequality, interviewees were far less supportive of the notion that government should redistribute income towards the less well off than was the general population. However, the latter were by no means egalitarians and the present interviewees may be closer to public opinion on this matter than is the case with privatisation and unemployment.

NOTES

1. For a discussion of the interviewees and interviews, see Appendices 1 and 2.
2. Before asking this question, the term 'progressive income tax' was clarified by explaining that it referred to a system in which those on higher incomes

paid a greater proportion of their income in tax than was the case with those on lower incomes. The clarification was to prevent any misunderstanding that the question referred to a radically egalitarian tax system. In fact, no one understood the term in the latter sense which would have led to ambiguity and confusion.

3. The shift between 1984 and 1985 amongst Conservatives and all respondents against the government's policy that the government should (a) give priority to the battle against inflation and (b) leave the market to sort out unemployment is evidenced by the results of Marplan poll findings (Reported in M. Linton, 'Cracks show in Tory convictions', *Guardian*, 4 October 1985). The table below (figures adapted from Linton's article) provides data on views about the statement at the head of the table.

'It's more important to control inflation than reduce unemployment.'

	Conservatives		All	
	1984	1985	1984	1985
Agree	59%	51%	35%	32%
Disagree	27%	38%	46%	57%

4. The Treasury estimated (May 1985) that 'The Government has paid out more than £173m in fees and commissions to banks, stockbrokers, accountants, and solicitors on the dozen major privatization issues since 1979.' (*Financial Times*, 25 May 1985). The Trades Union Congress in its publication *Stripping Our Assets: The City's Privatization Killing* asserts that the government and City have concealed the true extent of the City's gain: the TUC's estimate for the *total* to May 1985 was £274.52m and they claim that this is an understatement because certain figures could not be obtained (pp. 9–10). In addition, dealings in new issues both by City firms on their own behalf and as agents for others has been exceptionally profitable: this is partly the result of low issue prices of privatised firms allied to enormous over-subscription for the issues. As a result, new issues trade at a marked premium giving big gains to those who succeed in obtaining shares initially; another consequence is that there is rapid turnover of shares as some realise potential capital gains and others buy what they failed to obtain on subscription. Stockbrokers and other intermediaries earn commissions and fees from such transactions.

5. Wider share-ownership is a major aim of the Conservative government and is linked to the vision of a people's capitalism. See the text of The Queen's Speech (*Financial Times*, 7 November 1985). See also: M. Smith, 'Further state sales lined up' (*Guardian*, 18 July 1985) which reports a speech by John Moore, Financial Secretary to the Treasury, who mentions wider share ownership as an aim of the privatisation policy.

6. J. Vickers and G. Yarrow, *Privatization and the natural monopolies*. See, especially, chapter 5.

7. There are many opportunities to avoid income tax if you have a very high income: for example, the Business Expansion Scheme (BES) introduced by the Conservative government is a very popular means amongst City people to lessen the burden of income taxation. Financial journals and newspapers provide coverage of BES opportunities: for example, the

weekly *Investors Chronicle* has a section on BES in every issue. The *Financial Times* frequently includes advertisements about new or existing schemes. The Scheme is intended to encourage investment in new enterprises which need start-up or venture capital: the investor locks up capital for a minimum of five years but in return receives complete tax relief on the investment; thus a top rate tax payer – 60 pence in the £ – has (nett) to pay out only £2000 to invest £5000 because all the tax levied at the top rate can be reclaimed (60% of £5000 = £3000). On the other hand, the capital is tied up for five years; the firms chosen for investment may fail and even if they do not the capital invested might be stuck in the firm(s) for want of buyers – the latter is a danger often associated with investment in small and/or unknown firms.

8. Taped interview: 219.
9. Taped interview: 195.
10. Taped interview: 225.
11. Taped interview: 200.
12. Taped interview: 201.
13. See, for example: C. Huhne, 'The new Conservative myth about the workshy of Britain', *Guardian*, 10 October 1985. Huhne calculates that the true figure for the period just after the interviews ended, that is, early Autumn 1985 was over 3.8 million.
14. One of the remarks is worth noting here. A stockbroker said: 'I think it goes back to Mr Beveridge. I think we've had about 25 or 30 years of maleducation of simple people and they've grown to expect subsidy in huge forms . . . '.
15. A. Heath, R. Jowell and J. Curtice, *How Britain Votes*. The authors took great care to produce 'a representative sample of eligible voters in Great Britain at the time of the 1983 General Election' (p. 177).
16. *How Britain Votes*: p. 16.
17. *How Britain Votes*: p. 134 (Table 9.2).
18. *How Britain Votes*: p. 16.
19. *How Britain Votes*: p. 132 (Table 9.1).
20. K. Young, 'Shades of Opinion' in R. Jowell and S. Witherspoon (eds), *British Social Attitudes: the 1985 report*: p. 21. Young's data come from the overall survey of social attitudes to which 2200 respondents contributed in 1984.
21. K.Young, 'Shades of Opinion': p. 22.
22. A. Harrison, 'Economic Policy and Expectations' in R. Jowell and C. Airey, *British Social Attitudes: the 1984 report*: p. 63.
23. Trades Union Congress, *TUC SUMMARY of an Opinion Poll carried out for the TUC by NOP Market Research on PRIVATISATION AND PUBLIC OWNERSHIP*. NOP interviewed a quota sample of 1969 individuals of 15 and over in October 1986.
24. A. Harrison, 'Economic Policy and Expectations': p. 63.
25. M. Mann, 'Work and the Work Ethic' in R. Jowell, S. Witherspoon and L. Brook (eds), *British Social Attitudes: the 1986 report*: p. 28. Data were collected in 1804 interviews of 'adults aged eighteen or over living in private households in Great Britain' (p. 173).
26. Mann, 'Work and Work Ethic': p. 38 (Table 2.12).

27. P. Taylor-Gooby, 'Citizenship and Welfare' in R. Jowell, S. Witherspoon and L. Brook (eds), *British Social Attitudes: the 1987 report:* pp. 12–13; 3100 interviews were carried out although some questions in the survey were only administered to half the sample.
28. M. Mann, 'Work and the Work Ethic': p. 27.
29. A. Heath, R. Jowell and J. Curtice, *How Britain Votes*: p. 125 (Table 8.10N).

3 Markets

In a free economy, any market, in any commodity, be it vegetables, antiques or houses, must offer a choice and the prices within the market are determined ultimately by supply and demand. So it is with The Stock Exchange. It is simply a highly sophisticated market place where the traded commodity is stocks and shares.[1]

1 INTRODUCTION

In chapter 2, data were presented to demonstrate that the interviewees do indeed believe in markets as indicated by their answers to questions about privatisation, income taxation and policies to deal with unemployment. In this chapter the subjective meaning for interviewees of this belief in markets is explored.[2] Understanding the subjective meaning of markets is critical for a grasp of what a belief in markets means to these individuals. The concepts of 'markets' and ' financial markets' are examined in sections 2 and 3 respectively. Sociologists have paid little attention to markets, other than labour markets, and consequently most of the conceptual discussion below refers to the writings of non-sociologists. Among sociologists only Weber has made any real contribution to our understanding of markets. Section 4 deals with a crucial feature of the work carried out by participants in financial markets, namely, how they go about assessing likely movements in the markets. Finally, our grasp of the subjective meaning of markets to (professional) participants can be strengthened by an analysis of the goals of participants and accordingly section 5 is devoted to this matter.

2 MARKETS

The financial system in the United Kingdom, in the words of the Wilson Report,[3] 'is essentially a market system'. What is a 'market'? Donaldson's definition is useful[4]:

It is simply the bringing together of buyers and sellers – physically, by telephone or by some other form of contact. But whatever the circumstances, a key role is then played by the so-called price-mechanism.

Markets are means to distribute goods and services widely and this is as true of 'financial markets' as it is of product markets: 'The function of a market is to collect products from scattered sources and channel them to scattered outlets'.[5] This statement is true of both product markets (for example, sheet steel) and financial markets (for instance, the surplus funds of the individuals who deposit money with banks which, in turn, lend to borrowers).

The commodities distributed in a market are plentiful or scarce relative to demand. Prices play a key role in balancing the forces of supply and demand and are themselves determined by the relationship between supply and demand[6]:

Thus, if buyers wish to purchase more than sellers wish to supply, PRICE will rise. As a result of price rises, buyers reduce the quantities they wish to buy and sellers increase the quantities they wish to sell, until at some particular price these quantities are equal and the separate decisions of buyers and sellers are consistent. Similarly, if sellers wish to sell more than buyers are prepared to take, price falls causing sellers to reduce the quantities they wish to sell and buyers to increase the quantities they wish to buy, until the quantities are again equal and decisions are consistent.

Those who are able to supply similar goods, services or skills compete with each other. Competition is a further key feature of markets, as Weber notes[7]:

A market may be said to exist wherever there is competition, even if only unilateral, for opportunities of exchange among a plurality of potential parties.

Competition may exist among both those who supply and those who demand a particular commodity.[8]

Finally, participants in markets wish to sell (or buy) but at the highest (or lowest) possible price. Weber notes[9] that 'dickering [trade by bargaining – DL] and rational calculation' are central to the market. These features follow from the fact that self-interest, both of individuals and firms, is paramount.[10] Participants, guided by a rational-calculative orientation make judgements as to what prices and quality to offer or accept when communicating with potential counter-parties.

3   FINANCIAL MARKETS

Financial markets, whatever their specific features, are above all markets. Prices play a crucial role in balancing the forces of supply and demand. For a particular commodity, suppliers compete with each other and so do clients. Participants in these markets, like those in all markets, pursue self-interest (that of the firm and the individual). Potential suppliers and potential clients bargain over prices and terms. Everyone is dominated by the rational-calculative orientation: continuous calculation of costs, opportunities and profits is characteristic of individual participants and firms.

What, then, are the specific features of financial markets? First, as is the case in all markets, commodities are traded. However, in financial markets the commodities are not objects or services with a practical use. In the words of Geisst[11]: 'a financial market is an arena where financial instruments change hands'. For example, in a stock exchange the 'commodities' traded are pieces of paper, 'securities'; such securities represent a right to a share of profits (equities) or to interest payments (debentures). Bargaining revolves around the prices of securities and suppliers and clients respond to their conceptions of the demand relative to supply for the securities concerned. Similarly, in the wholesale money markets, borrowers (for example, a local council or an industrial corporation) will issue 'Paper' which stipulates the reciprocal rights and obligations of borrower and lender. The price (that is, interest rate) and terms (repayment dates, and so on) are determined by bargaining against the backcloth of a particular relationship between supply and demand. Both potential supplier and potential client compete with others for opportunities of dealing, that is, doing business: both parties must bear in mind the fact that usually there are others willing to take business from them if they do not offer competitive prices and terms. Furthermore, it must not be forgotten that the relationship between supply and demand changes continuously, often rapidly and frequently unpredictably in financial markets. Whether one is buying or selling or providing or consuming a service for a fee, all participants wish to profit by the transaction. Everyone is dominated by the rational-calculative concern with the exploitation of opportunities to make money.

Opportunities for gain in financial markets involve the manipulation of strictly financial means rather than a direct involvement in production, that is, acting on nature whether in its primary or partly transformed state. The manipulation of financial means focuses the minds of participants on a single (quantitative) feature of economic processes: profitability. Like all capitalists City firms and City people wish to make money but in the financial sector long processes of production do not intervene between investment and profit. The products of manufacturing and service industries are judged purely and simply in terms of the return on capital employed. Qualitative features of products are reduced to a quantity. City firms are themselves judged by this standard and they judge everything else in the same way. Furthermore, time-spans in the City are short because investors continuously compare returns over the period of a few months or a few years. In consequence, financial markets are dominated by a single criterion of economic success: short-term profits.

Why is this short-term view dominant? The answer is that financial markets are extraordinarily volatile and, as a result, participants have an immediate relationship to market forces.[12] For example, prices of most shares change constantly during the day while normally prices in a supermarket do not. In chapter 1, it was emphasised that financial markets are flex-price markets, that is, prices constantly change as buyers and sellers respond to the changing balance of supply and demand. Constantly changing prices expose participants directly and immediately to market forces on a continuous basis. Market-makers, the stall-holders in financial markets, from whom investors buy and to whom they sell (see Appendix 3), do not wish to tie up capital in holding stocks of equities, preference shares, foreign currency or whatever they deal in. They make profits from dealing and wish to clear their 'positions' (holdings) at the end of each day or short trading period. For example, the dealers in a small foreign owned bank were observed: from about 11.30 a.m. on the Friday (that is, at the end of a week's trading), they did not deal (for instance, borrow or lend foreign currencies for profit) but were concerned only to keep their positions in each currency as low as possible. Capital must always be working, never idle if there is a choice. Similarly, investors or their agents ('stockbrokers' and other 'brokers', for instance, foreign exchange brokers) are always responding to changing prices and returns on investment by selling, buying and switching investments. Overall, the daily work of City people exposes them to an exceptional degree to the immediate and sometimes brutal effects of market forces on a continuous basis. The reason for this exceptionally (as compared with product and non-financial service markets) direct or immediate relationship to market forces is the price volatility of financial markets. Participants are also exposed, although sometimes less than they would admit, to the cold winds of competition. Constant price changes in a competitive environment keep participants aware of their immediate relationship to market forces. Although, interviewees often referred favourably to the fact that the results of their efforts are immediately apparent (section 5), this feature of financial markets generates insecurity:

> The one obvious problem is that you are only as good as your last bargain. Each day starts a new, complete sheet. (Stockbroker)[13]

4 KEEPING IN TOUCH WITH THE MARKET

Surviving in a financial market (as in any market) depends upon keeping track of developments in the market. Keeping in touch is especially difficult in volatile markets where prices change all the time. In circumstances where one is constantly exposed to market forces, the cardinal condition for success – whether of individuals or firms – is an alertness to the indications which allow one to judge the balance of supply and demand at prevailing prices and to the signs of price changes in either direction. Dealers, that is, individuals who are reponsible for actually transacting the deals have to monitor prices continuously and be alert to signs that prices may be about to change. In market terminology, the dealer needs to 'keep in touch with the market'. Let us examine how jobbers (pre-Big Bang market-makers in The Stock Exchange) and stockbrokers (the agents for investors) managed to do so

Readers should note that, although the example comes from 1985, participants in all financial markets have to gather and assess information about markets, the forces that drive them and the requirements of investors. In these essential respects, the pre-Big Bang and post-Big Bang stockmarkets are similar.

Jobbers had to assess the balance of supply and demand and 'make prices' on the basis of their assessment of the state of the market. Like all market-makers they would quote a two-way price: the 'bid' at which they would buy and the 'offer' at which they would sell; market-makers aim to buy more cheaply than they sell but in volatile markets this is often difficult. Making prices is a matter of judgement about the likely balance of supply and demand at any specific price and success depends upon a detailed knowledge of what is happening in the market for the securities concerned. An enormous number of factors affected jobbers' decisions about what prices to make including recent experience in trading the particular security (for example, BT shares); press or 'tip sheet' comment[14] about firms or sectors; general conditions in The Stock Exchange and in other markets (for example, the foreign exchange market); the state of the domestic or international economy; political hopes and/or anxieties.[15] Jobbers – like all market-makers made most of their money by dealing rather than because the value of their holdings appreciated and, consequently, they were always ready to change prices to attract business. A flexible response to the forces of supply and demand in the market-place is required:

> A jobber who is short of stock may quote a price that is higher than the others. He will therefore attract any sellers, but not buyers, which is what he wants to do, because from his point of view, demand is exceeding supply. In the same way another jobber in the same stock may feel he has too many of a particular security and be willing to cut his price to attract buyers.[16]

A market-maker has to commit capital to the market: a holding of a particular security (or national currency, and the like) is termed a 'position' in that security (national currency, and so on). Clearly, 'taking a position' in a security exposes the market-maker to market forces. In a volatile financial market this meant that jobbers (like all market-makers) had constantly to assess the market and act accordingly. The net effect of a number of deals had to be monitored: that is, the senior jobber had to know exactly what the firm's position was in that security or overall range of securities traded. Details of every deal ('bargain') were noted in a loose-leaf book (contemporary market-makers hold the 'book' in computers): market-makers use the terms 'book position' or 'position' as synonyms. Jobbers (like all market-makers) made prices on the basis of a constant analysis of the position and the estimated P & L (Profit and Loss) of the 'pitch' (that is, team) both in specific lines of stock and in the whole range of stocks dealt with by the team. Market-makers can be 'long' of stock or 'short' of stock. 'Long' means that the market-maker holds the specific security and is looking for buyers. 'Short' means that the market-maker has sold stock which the firm does not already own: the market-maker has to buy stock before the delivery date. The jobber calculated P & L by adding up the profit and loss on deals transacted; an estimate was made for stock in hand by comparing the price at which stock was bought to an estimated price at which it could be sold (for a 'long position'); an estimate was made for the cost of buying stock (when the jobber had sold 'short') by comparing the price at which stock was sold to the estimated price of buying it before the date of delivery. The jobber as a market-maker had to make every effort to keep track of the firm's position and to improve it where necessary, otherwise tremendous sums of money could be lost quickly as prices moved in volatile markets:

> Now you've seen the pressure that we've had today. And I was very unresponsive to a lot – you were asking me questions. . . . I wasn't ignoring you. . . . I had a lot of things on my mind. I had a lot of big positions. . . . when, and especially at lunchtimes, when you have a moment to think, [you ask yourself:] 'Now where can I go with this? Where have I got to buy those?' That is the pressure you're living with. (Jobber)[17]

The need to keep track of capital and how effectively it is used is characteristic of any capitalist. In Weber's words[18]:

> Where capitalist acquisition is rationally pursued, the corresponding action is adjusted to calculations in terms of capital. . . . The important fact is always that a calculation of capital in terms of money is made . . . Everything is done in terms of balances: at the beginning of the enterprise an initial

balance, before every individual decision a calculation to ascertain its probable profitableness, and at the end a final balance to ascertain how much profit has been made.

For the capitalist in a financial market, calculations are continuous because prices change constantly.

The market-maker can only manage positions effectively and deal profitably if he or she is 'in touch with the market'. Keeping in touch requires the collection and assessment of information. Jobbers (like all market-makers) had means to gather market intelligence. Key among these were 'limit orders', that is, potential or conditional orders. The stockbroker (as agent for the investor) left information about potential deals with a jobber: for example, the stockbroker may have wished to buy shares which the jobber could not currently supply or the stockbroker's client would not sell at the prevailing price but would do so at a specified higher price. Limit orders allowed the jobber to assess which way the market might go: for example, the jobber would note a build-up of potential buyers and an absence of potential sellers of a specific 'line of stock'. The jobber used the knowledge provided by limit orders in the management of positions. For example, a jobber saw a build-up of potential sellers of shares in XYZ at a slightly higher bid price (that is, the price at which the jobber will buy stock) than she or he is making. Later, the jobber wishes to 'undo' a short position which left the firm dangerously exposed if prices of buying in stock rose. The jobber, therefore, sent a message to the stockbroker, who had left the appropriate limit order, that the firm would now buy at a higher (bid) price. The stockbroker was presented with a more attractive bid price equal to or near to the price earlier indicated as acceptable. The stockbroker responds, if necessary consulting the investor and often after a process of bargaining if one or either party feels that the terms of the deal can be improved. If the jobber was successful in buying the shares, the firm's exposure to the market had been reduced: the short position had been reduced or had even been 'undone' altogether. Changing prices also enabled the jobber to gather market intelligence because the response of stockbrokers and investors provides indications about 'the way the market is moving'. Usually the jobber changed prices to generate business. For example, the writer observed a team raising the bid price to encourage sellers of oil stocks on a slow afternoon. But sometimes prices were changed merely to assess the state of the market. A stockbroker described a jobbing practice known as 'shaking the tree': jobbers lowered bid prices to see how quickly sellers appeared when the bid price dropped; a rush of selling may indicate how many holders of the stock concerned were 'weak holders', that is, ready to sell quickly if prices 'eased' (that is, dropped slightly).

Stockbrokers also need to 'keep in touch with the market' in order to carry out their role effectively. Before Big Bang, stockbrokers were agents for investors: their income was derived from commissions paid by the investor when buying or selling. Except in carefully defined circumstances, they were prohibited from taking positions and making markets. Stockbrokers required two kinds of information: what their clients wanted and what was affecting the markets. They gained information about clients' needs and intentions by talking to them regularly or as often as necessary. Both when advising clients and when encouraging clients to deal, they required information about developments in relevant markets (that is, The Stock Exchange, stockmarkets abroad, foreign exchange and commodity markets), industrial sectors, companies and about wider trends (likely interest rate trends, rates of economic growth). Such information was supplied by 'analysts', who investigated particular sectors (for example, banks) and the companies in them, and by economists employed by stockbroking firms.

An analyst explained his work in these terms:

> What you've got to do is find shares that are going to go up. As a secondary – but very, very strong secondary – to that (I mean, even if shares don't go up) your estimates of what's going to happen inside the company has [sic] got to be dead right. So if shares go down, but the company makes a profit forecast you said it would make, that's O.K. You can say, 'Well, the market was against me but I've done all my homework. Look I'm not at fault. You should be happy: profits are going to carry on rising. Don't worry because the market will catch up sooner or later.' And there's . . . a terrific amount of pleasure in spotting something before anyone else does and having encouraging [sic] people to go into a share . . . and then seeing it, you know, being up fifty per cent, a hundred per cent. (Analyst)[19]

Although analysts sometimes spoke to institutional clients (for

instance, fund managers in pension funds), normally
'institutional salesmen' (usually called 'salesmen')[20] talked to the
institutional clients and private clients specialists to the
individual investors. Those who talked to clients required reliable
information and good advice from analysts and economists but
they had to assess what was supplied to them and package it for
the client. Clients needed to feel that the stockbroker 'got the
market right' as often as possible or they would be tempted to
desert the firm. Here is a salesman who specialises in Gilts (that is,
UK Government Securities) talking about the achievements
which give him pleasure:

> It's getting the market right. It's persuading somebody that
> there are reasons for doing something: be it buying, be it selling,
> be it switching [from one stock to another] defensively or
> aggressively. And finding that the market does do what you
> think it's going to do. You've made money for the firm through
> the transaction. You've also made money for the client. You've
> gained a bit of credibility. . . . I do genuinely feel quite proud
> when I've got something right for somebody. (Stockbroker)[21]

Making money for the client was essential; any intrinsic pleasure
derived by the salesman from his success was an extra.
Achievement of the former goal depended on constant assessment
of volatile financial markets and the factors driving them forward.

The role of the specialist stockbroking function known as the
'dealer' was also central to 'getting the market right'. The 'dealer'
had a dual role as someone who both executed deals and collected
information about matters such as prices, buyers, sellers and
rumours (takeovers, mergers, bankruptcies). Pre-Big Bang the
dealer (except those dealing in foreign securities) worked on the
'market floor', that is, the floor of The Stock Exchange. Both
clients and office-based colleagues (salesmen, private clients
specialists, analysts, economists) relied on the dealer for
up-to-date information about what was happening in the market.
Pre-Big Bang only dealers had access to 'real time' prices because
screen prices were always a few hours old and their duties
involved touring the 'pitches' (the stalls of jobbers) and noting
down prices and talking to jobbers about developments. What
jobbers said to dealers always had to be treated with caution since
they were on the other side (the buyer for your seller and vice
versa): jobbers wanted to persuade stockbrokers to deal on their
terms; what they said was information about the market which

had to be interpreted by the stockbroker to fit the needs of investors and stockbrokers. For example, a dealer referred to his early morning talk to jobbers: they claimed to speak objectively about what would happen in the market that day but, in fact, they were merely 'pumping out what they want to do in the first hour or so' and, consequently, he treated jobbers' remarks as 'spoof', that is, (attempted) deception.

Finally, we can most adequately grasp how stockbrokers learn about the market through the words of two participants. First, here is an experienced salesman speaking about how she and her dealers try to understand the market by watching other stockbrokers:

> Interviewer: 'How do you pick up your knowledge or your understanding of what the market's doing . . . ?'
> Interviewee: 'First hand, I suppose, it's through our own dealers who . . . will be moving round the floor and noticing that one particular dealer for another firm is constantly buying the same stock or what have you. So . . . we have to try and then find out. There's a lot of interest being generated in a particular stock and it's often . . . that another broker is pushing it and yet haven't yet got a note out on it [to the fund managers in the institutions – DL] . . . Maybe . . . [the analyst has] just been to see them [the company concerned] and has some more updated news than, perhaps, we have or other brokers have. It could be more meaningful than that – it could be that someone's . . . quietly building up a stake [possibly prior to a takeover bid]. But, I mean, nothing's done that quietly in the market. I mean buyers are noticed. (Stockbroker)[22]

Secondly here is a young dealer in equities talking about how he gains information from bargaining with and watching the jobbers:

> You watch and you get to know which people are doing what things. And you get to know which way the market's going by the feel of it. You can go into the market and know there's a lot of business going on just by the hum in the market . . . you can tell things by that . . . There are certain stocks – where you can pick 'em out – and, you see, if they move one way, the whole of that sector's going to move that way. And you build up your knowledge of the sector . . . and . . . you can check your prices and see which way the prices are moving so you know if there's

been buyers in there or sellers. And you get to know if there're short positions in the market and they're [that is, the jobbers – DL] being squeezed, and things like that.

Interviewer: 'How do you know when they're being squeezed?'
Interviewee: 'Well, the way the price moves so quickly.'

Further on he says:

It's all bluff and double-bluff. . . . I mean, if I go down to a jobber's pitch saying that I can pay fifty pence for a share, but I don't think it's worth paying fifty pence – I bid him forty seven pence for a stock even though I can pay fifty. He doesn't know I can. So, if he says, 'No, fifty's the price', I say, 'Well, fair enough, try me when you can show me the offer lower down . . .'. And he'll say 'We'll offer you stock at, say 48 but 47 is too cheap.' . . . The reason you bid him inside is because you either know that he's got a lot of stock or the way the stock has moved recently; or, you fancy the market's going to go easier so you bid him underneath. And he knows – he knows – as well the market's going to go easier so he'll deal with you. Because he knows once – the market's – it's gone easier, you'll bid him even lower still. But, if you see a turn in the market and you feel the market's going to go better, then you go to him and pay the price if you have to. (Stockbroker)[23]

The dealer is telling us about how, when negotiating with a jobber, he looks for signs about trends in the market. Similarly, he seeks for indications about the jobber's position: sharp price changes might indicate that the jobber is desperate to undo a deteriorating position.

5 GOALS OF PARTICIPANTS

Understanding markets involves more than a delineation of their characteristic 'objective' (impersonal) features. It is necessary to grasp the goals of participants. This section deals with competition and ambition in the City.

Understanding City people involves consideration of three matters. First, City people are competitive and extraordinarily ambitious for career advancement. Second, they are committed to earning exceptionally high incomes. Third, they gain great intrinsic satisfaction from their work. These matters are examined below.

(a) Competition and ambition

City people work in financial markets and they enjoy the competition between firms and between individuals. A commitment to competition is essential if one is to be effective in markets. The City person usually appears busy, which is important if you desire promotion and the associated higher income. This busyness is obvious to the outsider and can be explained either, as City people would, as the result of competition in high powered jobs or rather differently as a compulsive response to the pressures of financial markets.

Why is busyness compulsory and compulsive in the City? The answer to this question lies in a key feature of City life: competition. First, there is competition at an institutional level. Firms operating in the same market compete: for example, City merchant banks compete with each other and with foreign financial institutions to launch a new bond issue for a giant corporation; market-makers compete for business by making competitive prices for equities. Similarly, different organised financial markets compete: for example, The Stock Exchange (now called the 'International Stock Exchange') and LIFFE (London International Financial Futures Exchange) compete on currency options (a financial instrument providing protection against changes in the value of national currencies or providing an opportunity to speculate on movements in currency values). There is competition between different financial instruments: for example, equity investment versus depositing money in high interest money market accounts. Different financial centres (New York, London, Tokyo, Chicago) compete for business. To the outsider, the City often appears closed off, riddled with restrictive practices and barriers to real competition.[24] For the insider competition is a reality: profits and commissions are always at stake and survival and, perhaps, growth are the potential prizes. City people are living through a veritable sea change in which competition, both nationally and internationally, is fierce partly because of the new 'liberalised' economic order (for instance, abolition of exchange control) and partly because of the breakdown of many traditional divisions which inhibited competition (for example, divisions between banks and building societies and between stockbrokers and jobbers). Competition, survival, adaptability, growth are thus constant preoccupations for those in each firm and market.

There is a second side to competition in the City: competition between individuals.[25] People are remarkably concerned to achieve maximum individual success both in status and in earnings. Competition is partly expressed through what one earns:

> . . . people judge people by money: you know if you earn lots of money you must be good. Which isn't always the case, actually – lots of people earn lots of money and they're not much good. I mean, they just manage to live out a con for several years before they get tumbled. (Economist employed in stockbroking firm)[26]

Individuals are constantly aware that they are being assessed by competitors, colleagues and clients. In such circumstances, hard work is objectively necessary but the individual knows too that appearances matter. One must be seen to be hard at work, brim full of bright ideas. People everywhere are judged by appearances but in the conformist world of the City, the width of individual choice is normally narrow albeit that the occasional eccentric is tolerated. Continuous activity is almost compulsory if you wish to succeed. What is more, such activity becomes compulsive, that is, a means to still anxiety in volatile, competitive markets where loss of a job can be only a few days away if things go badly wrong. Furthermore, City people believe that one achieves results through energetic activity (they idolise the successful entrepreneur who has gone from a modest background to extreme riches, for example, Alan Sugar of Amstrad) – constantly trying out ideas, never giving up; you must achieve results if you are to be successful. In such an environment, someone who is obviously inactive is a matter of concern to others and could jeopardise her or his career as well as the work of the team on which individuals depend.

In merchant banks in particular and, to some extent, in stockbroking firms, the most ambitious not only work hard but also work long hours, staying in the office, almost as a matter of principle, until 7.00 p.m. or 8.00 p.m. even when there is no immediate need to do so. A middle-aged, rather successful, senior executive of a merchant bank referred to this habit with distaste:

he went home if there was nothing to do but some people merely stayed, he said, to be seen. The people he was criticising – very often young people who had not yet, unlike him, established themselves (he should soon be a main board director) – would claim that they stayed because it was necessary.

People spoke again and again of how hard they worked, what long hours they put in, how much pressure they were under. Two of the most ambitious and successful young people interviewed talked explicitly about the problems of being noticed. A young, desperately ambitious, woman merchant banker had joined the corporate finance division (advising corporations on strategy), unlike many women who go into the banking or investment management side, because the opportunities to progress to director are much greater there. She normally stayed at work until 8.00 p.m. and sometimes later and talked constantly about the need to appear as someone destined for success. She felt insecure and threatened because corporate finance is still largely the preserve of men, more particularly those from the major public schools (she had attended a highly regarded girls' public school). The problem in getting ahead, as she sees it, is that much of her work is research which often does not lead to observable results – corporate deals and so on. She feels that achievement in her work is 'diffuse' and is, therefore, not noticed; she complained that 'no one ever thanks her'.

A highly successful young jobber who, since the interview, has had a dramatic rise told me about his attempts to 'make a name' for himself. He was very aware of the need to achieve the kind of results which would impress senior people. He certainly seems to have achieved his aim, judging by the financial press publicity about his move (as part of a team deserting) to a rival firm for a steep rise in salary. These two individuals were particularly frank about their intentions and exceptionally ambitious even by City standards, but all the young people interviewed were remarkably ambitious.

Everyone who works in the markets is engaged in some form of selling: ideas, information, expertise, stocks and shares and other financial instruments, funds for borrowers and so on. Selling, in any context is notoriously insecure, because demand and competition are unpredictable. As a consequence, these ambitious individuals working in the financial markets are extraordinarily insecure both because of their ambition and because of the volatility of their markets. The insecurity of the two interviewees which has just been discussed is a manifestation of this general point. Selling is not merely a matter of selling some good or service: it is in large measure selling oneself as a reputable, competent and suitable person. Arthur Miller in *Death of a Salesman* captured the precariousness and transitory nature of success in selling:

> . . . Willy was a salesman. And for a salesman, there is no rock bottom to the life. He don't put a bolt to a nut, he don't tell you the law or give you medicine. He's a man out there in the blue, riding on a smile and a shoeshine. And when they start not smiling back – that's an earthquake.[27]

(b) High incomes

Coakley and Harris write:[28]

> The Square Mile of the City of London is a different world. Its exclusive concern is money and finance, and its workers, commuting from the suburbs, earn the wherewithal to set themselves apart from white-collar employees elsewhere.

The prize for the successful City person is a very high income. Indeed, 27 out of 97 interviewees who were asked what they liked about the job mentioned the high income provided. Here is one of the more articulate answers received:

> I like dealing with quite sophisticated people about quite sophisticated things. I like a job which carries a fair bit of responsibility with it and I'm very interested in being highly paid. (Senior Stockbroker)[29]

What is striking about City people is that individuals with relatively little management responsibility (they are not directors, partners, chairman) can earn enormous sums. Data on the earnings (usually 1984–85 financial year) of the 98 people in my sample are summarised in Table 3.1.

The following points emerge from Table 3.1:

People aged 30 and above: only 11 out of 54 earn less than £30 000; nine of the 11 earn £20 000–£30 000. Of the remaining two, one is a partner in a jobbing firm who normally would expect to earn

TABLE 3.1 *Breakdown of interviewees by earnings in 1984–85*

Earnings (£s)	All providing data	Each of the age groups			
		20–29	30–39	40–49	50+
Under 10 000	5	4	1*	0	0
10 000–19 999	13	12	0	0	1**
20 000–29 999	17	8	5	2	2
30 000–39 999	15	3	7	4	1
40 000–49 999	10	1	4	3	2
50 000–99 999	14	1	5	7	1
100 000+	9	0	2	3	4
Number providing data	83	29	24	19	11

*Partner in a firm which had a very bad year in 1984–85.
**Semi-retired Stockbroker; works to occupy himself and because he enjoys it.

around £75 000 (the firm had a poor year in 1984–85 but the future is now secure because a bank has bought the firm) and the other is a semi-retired Associate Member of The Stock Exchange who dabbles for interest and is a rich man.

People aged under 30: of the 29 people aged between 20 and 30, 13 earn over £20 000 (five over £30 000) and 16 less than £20 000; only four trainees earn under £10 000.

All individuals who provided adequate information: out of 83 people, only 35 earned under £30 000 and only 18 of the 35 earned under £20 000; of the 18 who earned under £20 000 all except two (one normally earning £75 000 – see previous paragraph – and the other a semi-retired rich man) are in their 20s.

Information is not available for 15 individuals. In four cases, interviewees were not asked about earnings: in three of these cases, there was someone else in the room for much of the time; in two cases (early interviews), the question about earnings was omitted in case the person found the question threatening. After these two interviews, the question about earnings was dropped to virtually the end of the interview in case it jeopardised the co-operation of interviewees. In fact, only one person explicitly objected to the question although some did refuse to answer it. In ten cases, interviewees declined to answer or said that they were only willing to give a vague indication which always turned out to be of no use. Two, of these (a director of one merchant bank and the chairman of another), almost certainly both earned well above £100 000 per annum. I estimate that, of the 15 who did not answer directly or fully: four or five earned well in excess of £100 000 (one or two might even have earned over £200 000 per annum) and three or four earned between £50 000 and £100 000 per annum.

Lest readers think that the salaries mentioned above are completely exceptional, John Moore (City Correspondent, *Financial Times*) in a 1985 article on the subject,[30] 'The dark cloud on the silver lining', discussed the recent explosion in City earnings for certain groups: market-makers generally and eurobond specialists in particular but also for other highly regarded individuals. He mentioned, as an example, a 21-year-old woman bond dealer who had taken a new job and seen her earnings jump from £21 000 to £50 000 per annum and states that 'a successful equity salesman who is not even a partner in a British securities firm can command as much as £170 000 in some cases'.

City salaries are high compared with non-manual earnings in other sectors of the British economy. The 1985 *New Earnings Survey*[31] shows that average earnings for the highest paid non-manual group, medical practitioners, are approximately £21 000. City professionals constitute a small proportion of the next best paid group ('Finance/tax specialists'). Evidence collected by *Income Data Services*, reported by Lloyd[32] about earnings in UK Merchant Banks shows average total cash earnings, for example, of a corporate finance executive at £32 000, of a senior corporate finance executive at £64 000 and of a head of mergers and acquisitions at £80 000. Dealers and traders have a lower status than those working in Corporate Finance and earn less.

Those in the highest positions often earn astronomical salaries. Moore, in the article referred to earlier, states[33]:

> In the past, senior partners in the top ten British securities firms were earning up to £1m a year each in a good year (of which there have been quite a few recently). Junior partners could be earning £80,000 to £100,000 each. Staff of broking firms, while not earning a very high basic salary, often under £20,000, would be receiving a bonus each year depending on how well the firm

has done. The bonus, calculated as a percentage of salary, might range between an extra 40 to 60 per cent.

Both Moore's and Lloyd's articles emphasise the recent surge in City earnings. Recently, as a result of the City 'revolution' and the concentration of the rapidly growing eurobond market in London (see Appendix 3) foreign securities firms (especially US and Japanese) have moved in force into London's financial markets. The competition between firms for scarce experience and talent in the area of market-making in general and of eurobonds in particular pushes staff salaries in these sectors skywards. Of course, this sharp upward trend in City salaries might not last, especially for those who are relatively less successful or are employed by the weaker firms.

(c) Intrinsic satisfactions

Participation in financial markets attracts those who are particularly motivated by exceptionally high financial rewards. It is not surprising therefore to discover that they enjoy the high income. However, there is more to their enjoyment of working in financial markets than earnings.

Interviewees were asked what they liked and disliked about their jobs. What was striking is that only one person out of 97 stated that there was nothing he liked about the job. Only two out of 97 expressed any marked dissatisfaction. Positive aspects mentioned outnumbered negative aspects by an enormous margin. Much of this job satisfaction was bound up with intrinsic features of the work carried out by the individual (excitement, using skills, and so on) and many mentions were made of liking colleagues and the City in general.

Much of what interviewees like about their jobs can be understood as a specific consequence of the fact that they work in financial markets (getting market right, enjoyment of dealing, the immediacy of the results of effort). City people are stimulated by the thrills of matching supply and demand and pitting their wits against the market. They like competition. They are subjectively attuned to markets: they live and breathe markets whatever their specialist functions (for example, analyst, dealer, salesman, merchant banker specialising in corporate finance, foreign exchange dealer). However, job likes were not always tied to the specific features of financial markets (for example, intellectual challenge, independence): Table 3.2 indicates the frequency of such job likes but these are not discussed because this section concentrates specifically on the subjective experience of financial markets.

In order to grasp the subjective meaning to participants of their work in financial markets, participants' concepts have, to a great extent, been used as the basis of the following analysis. For example, many interviewees actually stated that they liked 'Getting the market right' and this became one coding in the analysis of job likes. Of course, during the analysis of data, judgements have necessarily been made that various individuals, despite using different words, are talking about the same thing. For example, remarks about the 'elation' and 'excitement' of the work have been coded as referring to the 'Excitement' of working in financial markets.

Data on what people like about their jobs, 'job likes', are presented in Table 3.2. 'Job likes' are broken down into the following four categories: (a) Aspects of the work: 'Immediacy'; 'Using skills'; 'Independence'; 'Variety'; 'Excitement'; 'Enjoy dealing'; 'Like the pressure'; 'Miscellaneous Aspects' (various features of the work which are each mentioned less frequently than those explicitly identified).
(b) Colleagues: 'Able people'; 'Like the people/City'; 'Camaraderie'.
(c) Achievements: 'Getting market right'; 'Making money'; 'Making money for clients'. Interviewees also mentioned 'high income' which is discussed in section 4 above because it is not an intrinsic feature of the work.
(d) Other: job likes not otherwise categorised.

The first and third categories ('aspects of the work' and 'achievements') are of great significance because they indicate clearly how much job satisfaction is related to working specifically in financial markets; for this reason analysis is confined to these two categories. (The fourth category – 'other' – is residual and is of little interest here.)

Within each category, the most important job likes are distinguished. To clarify the meaning of each coding (for example 'Excitement'), appropriate quotations from interviews have been selected. Striking quotations – those which are most illuminating – rather than run-of-the-mill (more representative) ones have been chosen.

Numbers in Table 3.2 indicate the frequency of each 'job like'.

However, quantitative data should be treated with caution because they represent the end result of complex processes. The most important components of these processes are that, first, the answers to questions have had to be interpreted and such interpretation is inherently subjective and, second, the apparatus of coding used is a particular way of organising data. For example, the apparently simple statement that ten interviewees mentioned 'Immediacy' of results as a job like is the product of a specific interpretation of several answers to the question, the decision to treat the answers as similar and the use of a specific set of codings. These quantitative data, therefore, are no more than a rough-and-ready indication of the frequency with which particular items cropped up in interviews.

TABLE 3.2   *Job likes of interviewees*

Item mentioned favourably	Times mentioned
(a) *Aspects of the work*	
Excitement	34
Variety	27
Independence	19
Pressure	13
Intellectual challenge	12
Dealing	11
Using skills	11
Immediacy	10
Competitive	5
Miscellaneous aspects	15
(b) *Colleagues*	
Likes the people/City	25
Camaraderie	12
Able people	6
Energetic atmosphere	1
(c) *Achievements*	
High income	26
Making money	16
Getting market right	15
Making money for clients	1
Other	20
No job likes (explicit statement)	1
Individuals providing data	97

(a) Analysis of 'aspects of the work'

'Excitement' was the most frequently mentioned of job likes in any of the categories (34 mentions out of a total of 289 items coded). Excitement is a crucial feature of financial markets:

> I think the big excitement is that it is a market-place. And a market-place is about people buying and selling – not really about brokers manipulating the market or anything like that. In the end you've got to have the people to do the deal to make the market move and the investors sometimes find that difficult to see but in the end it's a supply and demand . . . I think it's really a question about trying to pit your wits against the information that's available . . . getting it right which is good news, getting it wrong which is disappointing but . . . we have got to make decisions all day long in one way or another – there is some excitement in it. (Stockbroker)[34]

A very senior jobber stated one reason why he liked the work:

> I 'spose really to sum it up, it makes the adrenalin flow. You can feel down in the dumps and then so elated it's not true . . . You get them wrong – of course, you get them wrong – and you do feel very depressed. But, my goodness, when it turns round! Every day is a new challenge. Every day is different. . . . You come in here and there's a lot of blue going 'round [a rising market – DL] and it elates you. Or, equally, if you come in and it's terrible day and you're a Bear [short of stock – DL] and you think, my God, . . . (Jobber)[35]

Clearly related to 'excitement' is the pleasure of 'dealing' which received 11 mentions. These remarks by the jobber just quoted show how closely the excitement of dealing in a financial market is bound up with competition between individuals, not just with the experience of betting against the market:

> . . . it's the challenge and it's winning really. And, that's winning making bargains – if you like, make [sic] a profit. I mean, I'm a committed capitalist obviously. . . . I suppose [a jobber is] like a bookmaker: he's making the odds because of supply and demand with the hope that he will make a profit . . . I suppose it's a bit of an ego-trip really – proving that you're a clever chap and you can . . . not beat the other man so much but win, perhaps, seven out of ten.

A number of people referred to the satisfaction gained from using their skills: 'using skills' was mentioned 11 times. This quotation comes from an interview with a partner in a stockbroking firm: his words demonstrate how the enjoyment of using skills is closely bound up for many City people with an enjoyment of competition:

> The satisfaction of analysis to me was simply the use of expertise and experience to make a competitive game. There's simply nothing more satisfying than to start with the same information as the . . . rest of the world and make a shrewder judgement – and profit at the expense of the rest of the world. . . . Not that you can do it very often. (Stockbroker)[36]

Not all mention of the pleasure of using skills or similar aspects referred to competition. For example, the appreciation of the intellectual challenge of some City work (coded 'Intellectual challenge') was not primarily about competition between individuals.

'Immediacy' was mentioned as a 'job like' by ten people, all of whom were either dealers or had been, or were very close to the dealing process. These are the words of a dealer on the floor of The Stock Exchange:

> In jobbing, particularly at the 'sharp-end' where you're actually the dealer, you have to make your mind up very fast and that immediacy appealed to me enormously. The nice thing about it also is that . . . there also is the opportunity to make considered judgements about the market but you have to be quite flexible about changing your mind because, in fact, the market isn't a logical, rational animal. It isn't something that you can actually be right about the whole time.(Jobber)[37]

Only five individuals explicitly mentioned liking the competitive nature of the work (coded 'competitive') despite the fact that this aspect was referred to when describing other positive aspects of their work: often interviewees merely stated that they liked the competitiveness of the job. Occasionally, they elaborated:

> I think probably you get a job satisfaction out of actually making money – your ability to – it's a question of everyday you're pitting your wits against other people. (Jobber)[38]

None of the aspects in the 'miscellaneous' category are of interest here.

(b) Analysis of 'Achievements'

Interviewees often answered the question about what they liked about their jobs by referring to 'Achievements', whether on behalf of the firm or by the individual concerned. The achievement of a high income was given great weight but since this was examined in section 5, it will not be discussed further at this point.

Much of what City people like about their work is that they make money for the firm. This aspect coded 'making money' was mentioned by 16 people. This statement by a young jobber is typical of views expressed by interviewees who were involved with dealing in one way or another (jobbers, dealers for stockbroking firms, salesmen, fund managers):

> . . . you buy a quarter of a million . . . [XYZ] and two minutes later you sell them tuppence higher – then that's five thousand pound profit and you've done that . . . And that's very satisfying. Of course, at other times they [his senior colleagues – DL] come back [from lunch and] you've done exactly the opposite and then you have to try'n and explain it [laughs]. But I mean, yeah, that's no trouble – it happens. There's nothing much you can do about it sometimes; it's a question not of how much you make but how little you lose.

At another point in the interview, he said:

> . . . I enjoy being down in the market. . . . But trading and taking a risk itself rather than [as a stockbroker does] puffing some poor client in or getting him out. I mean to me there's a lot of satisfaction if – as a jobber – you take a view and do something and it turns out right, then its P & L for yourself. Equally, if you do something wrong, you lose money yourself . . . (Jobber)[39]

A 'blue-button' (trainee) in a firm of jobbers put it this way: 'It's exciting. I mean when you actually see money being made for yourself. I find that quite exhilarating, you know'. (Jobber)[40]

The satisfaction of 'getting the market right' which was mentioned 15 times was dealt with in the earlier discussion of 'Keeping in touch with the market' and no more need be written than that success in getting the market right is both objectively desirable and subjectively satisfying. Subjective satisfaction cannot be reduced to the career requirements to be a successful judge of the market: there is intrinsic pleasure in being right.

The aspects coded 'other' are often of little interest because they could relate to any job, not just to one in a financial market. For example a dealer in a stockbroking firm likes the fact that his work is very mathematical. A manager in a stockbroking firm liked being part of a new outfit. A senior merchant banker liked contributing to the business. Someone in top management enjoyed helping to make his firm expand.

In summary, City people gain great intrinsic satisfaction from their work. This satisfaction is to a significant extent bound up with the volatile nature of financial markets and the immediate relationship of participants to market forces.

6   SUMMARY

This chapter analysed the concept of markets and drew attention to certain key features: supply and demand, the critical role of prices, the rational-calculative orientation of market participants and the competition which drives markets forward. The nature of financial markets was examined paying attention to their volatile character. The immediate relationship of participants to the market was explored and an attempt was made to explain the short-term orientation of participants in terms of the volatility of financial markets. The means by which market participants 'keep in touch with the market' in a context of constant price changes was described. Section 5 added to our understanding of financial markets by analysing the goals of participants from the point of view of the subjective meaning of their work. The attitudes of participants were analysed in terms of their ambition and competitiveness, both of which qualities conform closely to the whole ethos of the financial markets. The extraordinary commitment to high incomes was discussed and this casts further light on the goals (or motivations) of City people. Finally, the satisfaction of work in financial markets was described with particular attention to those job likes which are associated specifically with work in financial markets.

NOTES

1. Neil F. Stapley, *The Stock Market*: p. 13.
2. C. W. Smith's *The Mind of the Market* deserves mention at this point. Smith gathered data from participants in the New York Stock Exchange. The book is a sociological study of the subjective meaning of the stock market to participants. He focuses upon how participants make sense of market events in order to act in relation to them. He distinguishes between different perspectives on the market and the conflicting 'interpretations of market events which these varying perspectives generate' (p. 20). These perspectives are termed 'orientations' to the market and four are distinguished. First, there is the 'Fundamentalist/Economic' orientation which can be summarised by the phrase 'market values reflect economic values' (p. 33) such as the firm's profits, interest rates, and so on. Second, the 'Insider/Influence' orientation conceives market events in interpersonal terms: supply and demand factors resulting from the activities of powerful institutions and individuals are pinpointed (pp. 23 and 146). Third, the 'Cyclist/Chartist' orientation involves the belief that 'the market has a life of its own' (p. 48) and that it cannot be explained by reference to outside factors. Fourth, the 'Trader/Market Action' view stresses that understanding the market involves a 'feel' for the 'mood' of the market (p.58) and that this involves both intellectual and emotional skills. Smith's study differentiates between the different working orientations adopted by participants. The present study concerns itself with the basic conception of the market shared by all participants, whatever their orientations.
3. [Wilson] Committee to Review the Functioning of Financial Institutions, *Report*: para. 106.
4. P. Donaldson, *A Question of Economics*: p. 119.
5. J. Robinson and J. Eatwell, *An Introduction to Modern Economics*: p. 148.
6. G. Bannock et al., *The Penguin Dictionary of Economics*: pp. 348–349.
7. M. Weber, *Economy and Society*, i: 635.
8. Restrictions upon competition are examined in chapter 1, footnote 6.
9. Weber, *Economy and Society*, i: 639.
10. Weber, *Economy and Society*, i: 43.
11. C. R. Geisst, *A Guide to the Financial Markets:* p. 1.
12. See S. G. Checkland, 'The Mind of the City 1870–1914' in *Oxford Economic Papers*, Vol. 9, 1957, pp. 261–78. My attention was drawn to passages on pp. 265 and 270 by G. Ingham's *Capitalism Divided?*: p. 242.
13. Taped interview: 139.
14. Tip sheets are circulars which claim to give high quality advice about under-rated or over-rated shares or about the future trading possibilities for particular shares. According to a jobber who was interviewed, tip sheets have most effect on 'illiquid' stocks, that is, those which are irregularly traded. In such stocks (shares, debentures), buying or selling interest will move prices rapidly.
15. For a list of relevant factors, see: G. Cummings, *Investor's Guide to the Stock Market*: p. 78. A market-maker in the eurobond market mentioned that the prices the market-maker makes are 'subject to many elements: supply and

demand, the quality of the paper [the security], and the 'position', further technical aspects of the market for the issue – all these in combination' (Taped interview: 149).

16.   The Stock Exchange (Information and Press Department), *The Stock Exchange*: p. 18.
17.   Taped interview: 191.
18.   M. Weber, *The Protestant Ethic and the Spirit of Capitalism*: p. 18.
19.   Taped interview: 157.
20.   This is the term used in the market both for men and the increasing number of women so engaged.
21.   Taped interview: 140.
22.   Taped interview: 229.
23   Taped interview: 212.
24.   For different views on this institutional level of competition, see: W. M. Clarke, *Inside the City*: chapter 16; H. McRae and F. Cairncross, *Capital City*: pp. 247–51. Clarke believes the City pre-Big Bang was competitive. McRae and Cairncross emphasise the barriers to competition. While the latter are correct in their concern with restrictive practices, the City has become more competitive in the 1980s.
25.   Pearson Phillips, *YAPs: The complete guide to Young Aspiring Professionals* is an amusing discussion of ambition and competitiveness among groups working in the city, advertising, and the like. A merchant banker originally drew the writer's attention to what he termed the 'self-oriented' nature of City people.
26.   Taped interview: 147.
27.   Arthur Miller, *Death of a Salesman*: p. 111.
28.   J. Coakley and L. Harris, *The City of Capital*: p. 1.
29.   Taped interview: 200.
30.   *Financial Times*, 31 July 1985.
31.   Reported by P. Bassett, 'Doctors head non-manual pay league with £400 average', *Financial Times*, 30 October 1985.
32.   IDS Top Pay Unit, October 1985: reported by J. Lloyd, 'Surge in City earnings "set to continue"', *Financial Times*, 9 October 1985.
33.   *Financial Times*, 31 July 1985.
34.   Taped interview: 177.
35.   Taped interview: 141.
36.   Taped interview: 188.
37.   Taped interview: 134.
38.   Taped interview: 169.
39.   Taped interview: 200.
40.   Taped interview: 182.

4 Explaining the City Belief in Markets

1 INTRODUCTION

This chapter is an attempt at a tentative explanation of the strong commitment of City people to the market. The argument developed is that the influence of social class, although relevant and important, is not alone sufficient to explain the City belief in markets because City people from modest backgrounds do not seem significantly less pro-market than those from the more privileged backgrounds. Attention must also be paid to the following: beliefs about the market held by recruits prior to entry into the city; the effect of working in financial markets; and the ideologically closed character of City culture. Each of these factors plays a crucial role in constituting and reinforcing socio-political opinions, including views about the proper relationship between state and market.

Section 2 examines the prior orientations of City recruits through the indirect evidence provided by a comparison of the views of older and younger people. An examination of data suggests that recruits enter with strong pro-market views which may then be reinforced by forces acting within City life. One of the major factors affecting prior orientations of recruits is social class background which is discussed in section 3. In section 4, the working context of financial markets which nourishes and sustains pro-market views is briefly examined – briefly because much of the relevant material has already appeared in chapter 3. In section 5, evidence about the closed ideological nature of the City is examined.

2 PRIOR ORIENTATIONS OF CITY RECRUITS

Only individuals already occupying positions in the City were interviewed. Consequently, the research provides no direct evidence about the beliefs held about the market prior to entry into the City. However, an indirect method has been used here to

81

assess whether City recruits arrive holding pro-market views: a comparison of the youngest age group (those under 30) with the rest (those over 30) which should indicate whether commitment to the market is greater among older groups, the members of which have presumably been in the City on average longer than those under 30. Although it is not possible here to control for length of time in the City (individuals start at different ages), the comparison provides evidence about whether pro-market views are merely the result of forces acting within the City and financial markets or whether recruits enter with strong pro-market views.

As explained in chapter 2, opinions about progressive income tax and privatisation are good indicators of views about the market. In Tables 4.1 and 4.2 views about both matters are broken down by age.

TABLE 4.1   *Views of progressive income tax: breakdown by age*

Age group	Opinion about progressive income tax			
	Favours strongly	Favours weakly	Opposes	Other
20–29	19 (63%)	5 (17%)	5 (17%)	1 (3%)
30–39	11 (50%)	6 (27%)	4 (18%)	1 (5%)
40–49	14 (61%)	6 (26%)	2 (9%)	1 (4%)
50+	8 (61%)	2 (15%)	1 (8%)	2 (15%)
No. & (%) holding each view	52 (59%)	19 (22%)	12 (14%)	5 (6%)

In Table 4.1, of those aged 20 – 29, individuals coded 'Favours Weakly' claim to favour progressive income tax but express significant doubts about the system existing in 1984–85 (chapter 2). The 'Favours Weakly' individuals do not really support even the mildly progressive income tax of 1984–85 – the formal progressiveness of which is undermined by the impact of tax avoidance schemes for the rich and better off. These interviewees together with those coded 'Opposes' constitute 33 per cent of those aged 20 – 29. Although the majority accept progressive income tax as it existed in 1984–85, the dissenters are a sizeable minority. Among those aged 30 and over, 39 per cent either have doubts about the existing system of progressive income tax or directly oppose it. However, there is no clear association between age and doubts about (coded 'Favours Weakly') or opposition to progressive income tax (coded 'Opposes'). The percentages in each group are: 20–29, 33 per cent; 30–39, 45 per cent; 40–49, 35 per cent; 50+, 23 per cent.

Table 4.1 shows that over a third of the youngest age group hold such strongly pro-market views that they either wholly reject or cannot accept without reservation even the very mildly progressive income tax of 1984–85 and this at a time of steeply rising City salaries. If we compare those aged 20 to 29 with those aged 30 and over, it seems that a longer period working in the City does not markedly shift opinions about progressive income tax in a pro-market direction.

However, opinions about the privatisation programme seem, unlike those about progressive income tax, to support the argument that individuals who are older, and have presumably on average spent more time in the city, more frequently hold the strong pro-market view that the state should keep out of industry. Data are presented in Table 4.2.

TABLE 4.2   *Opinion about privatisation: breakdown by age*

| Age group | Opinion about Privatisation | | | |
	Favours	Mixed	Opposes	Other
20–29	21 (70%)	7 (23%)	2 (7%)	0 (0%)
30–39	19 (79%)	2 (8%)	3 (12%)	1 (4%)
40–49	20 (77%)	4 (15%)	2 (8%)	0 (0%)
50+	12 (86%)	2 (17%)	0 (0%)	0 (0%)
No. & (%) holding each view	72 (76%)	15 (16%)	7 (7%)	1 (1%)

The Table shows that support for privatisation is the City orthodoxy; those not wholly supporting the programme, as noted in chapter 2, seldom express outright opposition: only seven out of 95 who expressed clear views claimed to oppose the policy. The lowest percentage of supporters of the policy are found in the youngest age group: this is compatible with the view that, although recruits enter with strong pro-market views, length of time working in the City is associated with the driving out of either the few heterodox views in individual minds (in this case, opposition to privatisation) or the individuals that hold these ideas.

In sum, data about the views of interviewees about progressive income tax and privatisation, broken down by age, suggest that City recruits arrive with pronounced pro-market views and that subsequent City life has a relatively less significant effect than influences acting prior to entry.

3   SOCIAL CLASS AND THE FORMATION OF PRO-MARKET VIEWS

To what extent are pro-market views determined by social class origins? Data presented below suggest that those from less privileged backgrounds do not necessarily favour market solutions less often than those from more privileged backgrounds.

The social class of origin of individuals has been determined on the basis of two indicators: first, type of school attended and second, father's occupation in terms of the Office of Population Censuses and Surveys (OPCS) classification.[1] Type of school attended is probably a more useful indicator of privileged versus modest class origins in the present context because the OPCS classification of social class includes under Social Class 2 occupations which are significantly different. For example, Social Class 2 occupations include owners of medium-sized and large firms as well as the lower professions such as schoolteachers. In fact, owners are members of the dominant class in a society based on private enterprise while teachers are members of an intermediate class between owners, higher managers, administrators and higher professionals on the one hand and routine white-collar workers and the manual working class on the other.

If social class were the major factor constituting opinions on state and market, we should expect individuals from the more privileged classes (1, 2 and 'Officer') to opt more often for the pro-market views: that is, to be both more hostile to progressive income tax and more favourable to the privatisation policy. Data about progressive income tax are presented in Tables 4.3 and 4.4 respectively. Data about privatisation are presented in Tables 4.5 and 4.6.

TABLE 4.3   *Opinions about progressive income tax: breakdown by father's occupation*

Father's occupation: OPCS Social class	Opinions about progressive income tax			
	Favours strongly	Favours weakly	Opposes	Other
1	12 (71%)	3 (18%)	0 (0%)	2 (12%)
2	17 (55%)	8 (26%)	5 (16%)	1 (3%)
'Officer'*	3 (50%)	2 (33%)	1 (17%)	0 (0%)
3N	6 (60%)	2 (20%)	2 (20%)	0 (0%)
3M	8 (57%)	3 (21%)	3 (21%)	0 (0%)
4	—	—	—	—
5	0 (0%)	1 (50%)	1 (50%)	0 (0%)
No. & (%) holding each view	46 (58%)	19 (24%)	12 (15%)	3 (4%)

*Interviewees whose fathers held positions as officers in the armed forces have been coded separately. OPCS does not allocate such individuals to a social class.[2]

It is instructive to compare the views of individuals from 'privileged' social class backgrounds (OPCS Social Classes 1 and 2 and 'Officer' group) with the views of those from 'modest' social class backgrounds (OPCS Social Classes 3N, 3M and 5 – there are no interviewees from Social Class 4). The interviewees themselves would be classified under OPCS Social Classes 1 or 2 depending on the specialist functions which means that those with fathers classified as belonging to Social Classes 3N, 3M and 5 have experienced upward social mobility. It should be noted that, although OPCS Social Class 2 includes a disparate range of occupations, including the lower professions, less than a quarter of interviewees with fathers classified Social Class 2 can be considered to have experienced upward social mobility: 28 of the 37 individuals (76 per cent) from Social Class 2 backgrounds have fathers who were in business as directors, owners of firms, stockbrokers, and so on rather than being members of the lower professions.

A lower proportion of individuals from more privileged social class backgrounds than from more modest backgrounds, express doubts about or oppose progressive income tax outright. Thirty-five per cent from Social Classes 1 and 2 and the 'Officer' group expressed doubts or opposition to progressive income tax while 46 per cent of Social Classes 3N, 3M and 5 did so. The latter are, despite their class origins, less supportive of progressive income tax; perhaps, this is scarcely surprising when one remembers that these interviewees are upwardly mobile and would claim to have gained success by their own efforts despite their origins.

Data in Table 4.3 support the argument that social class is not the main factor contributing to the pro-market views of interviewees. Furthermore, the breakdown by type of school attended in Table 4.4 supports this argument.

TABLE 4.4   *Opinions about progressive income tax: breakdown by school type*

Type of school attended	Opinions about progressive income tax			
	Favours strongly	Favours weakly	Opposes	Other
Private*	25 (60%)	10 (24%)	4 (10%)	3 (7%)
Maintained**	13 (45%)	8 (28%)	7 (24%)	1 (3%)
No. & (%) holding each view	38 (54%)	18 (25%)	11 (15%)	4 (6%)

*Includes two individuals attending overseas schools similar to British 'public schools'. Excludes three individuals who attended Direct Grant Schools because in such schools some parents paid fees and others did not.
**Excludes individuals who attended Direct Grant Schools for reasons explained above.

Table 4.4 shows that when social class origin is categorised by reference to type of school attended, we find that once again those from more 'modest' backgrounds (Maintained Schools) are less supportive of progressive income tax (52 per cent express doubts or opposition) than those from more 'privileged' backgrounds (Private Schools), only 33 per cent of whom express doubts or opposition. This means that individuals from modest backgrounds are more likely than those from privileged backgrounds to believe that the distribution of income produced by market processes should not be altered even mildly, by taxation.

Overall, with respect to opinions of progressive income tax, social class of origin has the opposite association with pro-market views to that one would expect if social class of origin were the

TABLE 4.5   *View of privatisation: breakdown by father's occupation*

Father's occupation: OPCS social class	View of privatisation policy			
	Favours	Mixed view	Opposes	Other
1	16 (84%)	1 (5%)	1 (5%)	1 (5%)
2	28 (76%)	7 (19%)	2 (5%)	0 (0%)
'Officer'	6 (100%)	0 (0%)	0 (0%)	0 (0%)
3N	7 (70%)	3 (30%)	0 (0%)	0 (0%)
3M	9 (75%)	1 (8%)	2 (17%)	0 (0%)
4	—	—	—	—
5	2 (100%)	0 (0%)	0 (0%)	0 (0%)
No. & (%) holding each view	68 (79%)	12 (14%)	5 (6%)	1 (1%)

TABLE 4.6   *View of privatisation policy: breakdown by school type*

Type of School attended	View of privatisation policy			
	Favours	Mixed view	Opposes	Other
Private*	38 (83%)	6 (13%)	1 (2%)	1 (2%)
Maintained**	23 (64%)	6 (17%)	6 (17%)	1 (3%)
No. & (%) holding each view	61 (74%)	12 (15%)	7 (9%)	2 (2%)

*Includes two individuals attending overseas schools similar to British 'public schools'. Excludes three individuals who attended Direct Grant Schools because in such schools some parents paid fees and others did not.
**Excludes individuals who attended Direct Grant Schools (see * above).

dominant factor constituting the views interviewees held about the market.

Opinions of privatisation are also a useful indicator of pro-market views. Tables 4.5 and 4.6 present the breakdown of views of privatisation by father's social class and type of school respectively.

Table 4.5 indicates that 81 per cent of individuals from Social Classes 1, 2 and the 'Officer' group express the pro-market view, support for privatisation, as against 75 per cent for those from Social Classes 3N, 3M and 5. Both groups include very high proportions of individuals who are opposed to state ownership of industry, but there is a slightly higher proportion in the former group.

Table 4.6, on the other hand, gives a more clear-cut indication that a privileged social class of origin is clearly associated with pro-market views. Eighty-three per cent of those from privileged backgrounds (Private School) favour the pro-market view compared to only 64 per cent of those from more modest backgrounds (Maintained School).

Overall, on the issue of privatisation, the breakdowns by type of school and father's social class both suggest that a higher percentage of those from more privileged backgrounds hold the pro-market view.

To summarise, analysis of views about progressive income tax suggest that 'modest' social class origins are associated more strongly with pro-market views than are 'privileged' origins. However, analysis of views about privatisation suggest that privileged social class origins are more strongly associated with pro-market views than are modest origins. There is no evidence of a clear association between social class of origin and views about the proper relationship between market and state.

4 HOW WORKING IN A FINANCIAL MARKET NOURISHES PRO-MARKET VIEWS

Working in financial markets breeds tremendous commitment both to the job and to the market mechanism in general. In chapter 3 the subjective meaning of work in financial markets was analysed. Virtually everyone interviewed stated that he or she liked the work. Much of what they liked about their jobs related to the specific features of financial markets.

How does job satisfaction breed and sustain belief in the market? First, financial markets strongly encourage pro-market views because, in this environment, participants see success rewarded and failure penalised. Participants believe that competition for business in financial markets stimulates hard work and new ideas. Commitment, effort and intelligence are so obviously rewarded in financial markets that it is very easy for participants to generalise the lessons learnt to all economic sectors in all countries. Overall, their working experience of markets nourishes and strengthens the positive attitude to the market which recruits held on entry.

Second, their experience of individual success, in the form of extremely high salaries and in some cases upward social mobility, has led to a strengthening of what were, even at the time of recruitment, pronounced pro-market views. Here we confront a 'material' cause: exceptional economic rewards, career advancement, a desirable social position and, occasionally, some managerial power are sound reasons for believing in the efficiency of market forces.

5 CITY CULTURE AND THE PROMOTION OF BELIEF IN THE MARKET

Chapter 2 provided evidence of the pro-market views of interviewees. What is the context within which such homogeneity of ideology grows? The answer is that City culture stifles dissent and consequently positively promotes the reproduction of pro-market views.

City people are not free to make up their own minds about the virtues of the market. There are covert pressures on recruits to City life. Socialisation pressures in the City are extraordinarily intense and there exists great intolerance of deviance on what is effectively a fundamental tenet of City life. Paul Ferris's comment,[3] made over a quarter of a century ago, about senior City people is still apposite and applies equally throughout the hierarchy:

> There are Left-wing people at self-employed and boardroom levels in the City; but not many, and they keep it to themselves. To be a responsible person in the City is to be automatically of the Right . . .

It is not merely that City life exudes the notion of the essential rightness of pro-market views. City people cannot really understand how anyone can be anti-market: it does not make sense to be unless you are against 'freedom of the individual' and 'enterprise'. A merchant banker remarked to the writer that 'Governments don't make a difference'. What he means is that markets will work as markets work whatever governments intend.

Markets are the way of the world and there is nothing one can do about it.

City life, like all ideologically closed worlds, provides each trainee with an intense period of socialisation. Suppression of doubt is intrinsic to the dynamics of socialisation[4] but most occupations allow some diversity, some questioning. City culture is dominated by the values and beliefs of the wealthy and the wealthy normally favour private ownership and the market. Furthermore, City culture is extraordinarily intolerant of dissent like certain other occupational groups, for example, the police and the armed forces. The trainee who doubts knows: 'I have two choices: get out or shut up'. Future research on individuals who decided to get out would be valuable. In the absence of such data, one must rely upon the testimony of those who remain and shut up (or keep rather quiet), such as the following examples. A market-maker stated that he supported progressive income tax because those who could afford to bear the burden should do so. He continued (referring to his colleagues): 'I'd probably get killed if you tell them I said that . . . [Laugh]'. A fund manager (managing unit trusts), who is a strong egalitarian, said when interviewed that he had given up discussing politics with his colleagues because it was so unpleasant to do so. A foreign exchange broker, who had been a Labour Party member and still described himself as a socialist, replied when asked whether he was still a member, 'How could I be and do this job?'.

Each example demonstrates the intolerance of City people of criticism of the market. What makes these examples even more telling is that none of these individuals is particularly left-wing. One voted Conservative in 1983 and the other two are mainstream Labour supporters.

Non-conformists in the City, therefore, normally keep quiet. However, the problem for the silent non-conformist is that silence reinforces and contributes towards the reproduction of the consensus which she or he finds so stifling. The dissenter faces a vicious cycle of conformity. The result is that within the City dissenting voices are seldom heard. Furthermore, outside critics can be written off as individuals who either do not understand financial (and other) markets or are opposed to capitalism and, therefore, deeply prejudiced.

A consideration of data collected about the newspaper and periodical reading habits of interviewees, presented in Table 4.7, provides a further indicator of the closed character of City culture.

TABLE 4.7   *Newspaper and periodical reading habits*

Newspaper or Periodical	Number of mentions
Daily Papers*	113
Times	38
Daily Telegraph	31
Mail	22
Guardian	12
Other daily papers	10
Weekly Periodicals**	50
Economist	34
Private Eye	12
Spectator	4
Sunday Newspapers	151
Sunday Times	50
Observer	38
Sunday Telegraph	33
Mail on Sunday	17
Sunday Express	6
Other Sunday Paper	7
Number of interviewees for whom data available	82

*The *Financial Times* is excluded because it is required reading for virtually everyone.
**This category includes periodicals with a political content (that is, leisure interest magazines are excluded) but excludes purely financial periodicals (for example, *Financial Weekly*).

It is apparent from Table 4.7 that almost everyone interviewed reads the national daily morning newspapers which are usually regarded as right-wing. There were 113 mentions of national daily morning papers. The *Guardian*, which is a little to the left of centre, appears 12 times compared with 38 mentions for *The Times*, 31 mentions for the *Daily Telegraph* and 22 for the *Mail*. Among the 12 *Guardian* readers are six of the small minority of non-Conservative voters interviewed (see chapter 5). One of the remaining six reads the *Guardian* purely for market information: this means that only five of the Conservative voters expose themselves to the *Guardian* on a daily basis.[5]

The data for Sunday newspapers are more difficult to analyse: the large number of *Observer* readers is striking. It appears that this liberal-minded newspaper is read for its excellent business section and other features rather than because it provides a balance to, for example, the *Sunday Times* and the other right-wing Sunday newspapers.

Among weeklies, many individuals mention the *Economist* which is an establishment right-wing weekly. *Private Eye* is popular but, although at times anti-establishment, cannot be regarded as having even mildly left-wing sympathies. Few people read the *Spectator* and none read the left-wing *New Statesman* on a regular basis, although one person stated that he read it occasionally.

Overall, data about regular reading habits are an indicator of how little contact interviewees have with opinions other than those which are strongly pro-market. Reading habits help to reinforce and perpetuate their uncritical pro-market views.

In summary, this section describes how individuals, after recruitment to the City, are subjected to massive pressures to conform to the overwhelming pro-market ideology. Such conformity reinforces the prior pro-market orientations of almost all recruits: social class origins may be wider than is commonly supposed but in terms of ideology the City recruits a very homogeneous set of individuals to career positions.[6]

6   SUMMARY

The chapter discusses some of the factors which are involved in the formation of the pro-market views of City people. First, the breakdown by age suggests that working in the City does no more than strengthen pre-existing pro-market views. Second, social class is not the crucial factor in forming pro-market views because individuals from 'modest' social class origins display similar views to those from 'privileged' backgrounds. These conclusions about social class apply whether father's occupation or type of school attended is taken as the indicator of class background. Third, the experience of working in financial markets appeared to encourage strong pro-market views because individuals perceive such markets as supremely efficient and generalise their experience to all economic sectors. Finally, the intolerant character of City culture encourages conformity and makes dissent difficult if not impossible.

NOTES

1. Office of Population Censuses and Surveys, *Classification of Occupations 1980*: especially pp. v-xiii.
    The following list of characteristic occupations classified under each social class is drawn from an examination of the above publication (see pp. x-xi and Appendix B).

OPCS Social Class	Characteristic Occupations
I	Higher professionals, senior government administrative staff
II	Intermediate occupations: schoolteachers managers in industry and transport, welfare workers.
III	Skilled Occupations (N) *non-manual*: for instance, supervisors in offices, clerks, secretaries, shop assistants (M) *manual*: for example, foremen, skilled manual workers (bricklayers, and so on)
IV	Partly skilled manual occupations: caretakers, dry cleaners, gardeners
V	Unskilled manual occupations: dockers, labourers.

    Officers in the armed forces are classified separately in the present study: OPCS does not classify them by Social Class. See p. lxxxviii.
    Interviewees were asked the occupations of their mothers but many were housewives and, in terms of the OPCS classification, could not be allocated to a social class. Therefore analysis had to be in terms of father's occupation.
2. See footnote 1.
3. P. Ferris, *The City*: p. 8.
4. I am grateful to Andrew Graham, Balliol College for this point.
5. *The Independent* had not yet been launched.
6. Data presented earlier in the chapter demonstrate that the City recruits far more widely than is commonly assumed. This fact scarcely matters if those from 'modest' social class backgrounds share the pro-market views dominant in the City.

5 City Ideologies

> The more pure and limited capitalist viewpoint is at its most trenchant and pervasive in the City. – R. Spiegelberg[1]

1 INTRODUCTION

In chapter 2 evidence was presented about the strong pro-market beliefs of interviewees. This chapter explores the major implication of these beliefs, namely the adherence of most interviewees to ideologies close to or consistent with Neo-liberalism. In order to demonstrate that Neo-liberal ideology plays this dominant role in the City, it is necessary first to discuss relevant theoretical concepts and certain issues of method.

Section 2 briefly examines the basic analytical concepts of this chapter: 'ideology' and 'ideal-type'. Section 3 outlines a typology of ideologies. The main elements of the four ideal-typical ideologies, Neo-liberalism, Traditional Conservatism, Liberal Democracy and Democratic Socialism, which are used in the analysis of interview data are described. Section 4 begins with an outline of the opinions on the interview topics associated with each ideal-typical ideology as a prelude to a discussion of the allocation of interviewees to ideologies. This section surveys the problems encountered during the process of allocating interviewees to ideologies before the results of the allocation are presented. Section 4 concludes with a discussion of the breakdown of interviewees, as classified by ideology, in terms of age. Section 5 presents case-studies illustrating each ideological standpoint.

2 BASIC CONCEPTS: 'IDEOLOGY' AND 'IDEAL-TYPE'

Classification of individuals by ideologies requires a framework of concepts within which classification can take place. Two concepts are basic to this analysis: 'ideology' and 'ideal-type'.

(a) Ideology

The concept of 'ideology' is here understood to refer to any reasonably coherent set of beliefs about the nature of the social world.[2] An ideology will incorporate views about the nature of the 'good society'; it will contain views about the obstacles to the realisation of the 'good society'. It will encompass general beliefs about a range of matters: for example, God; how we should live; sexual morality; the family; property; equality and inequality; the nature of human freedom. In a society like Britain in the 1980s, significant ideologies will include views about the actual and desirable roles of the state, the nature of the market, the desirability of greater equality and the conditions for freedom. This study focuses upon the matters outlined in the previous sentence rather than upon the broader issues listed in the penultimate sentence.

In this study, the use of the term 'ideology' to refer to a specific constellation of beliefs does not necessarily imply that the constellation so described fundamentally distorts reality or is one-sided and partial, although ideologies often (perhaps, always) do suffer from such defects. The overall purpose of the chapter is to allocate interviewees to ideologies rather than to subject each ideology to sustained criticism.[3] Criticisms of certain key beliefs associated with the dominant ideologies of the City, such beliefs being held by the vast majority of interviewees, will be found in chapters 1 and 2.

(b) Ideal-types

What is an 'ideal-type'? Max Weber emphasised three features.[4] First, an 'ideal-type' is a theoretical construction. Theory can never be merely a copy of empirical reality because reality is infinite and can never be grasped as a whole. Sociological analysis, like all human thought, abstracts from reality.[5] Sociologists select what is significant for their research. Second, because the ideal-type is a theoretical construction, the justification for using it is not that it describes reality but that it has a heuristic value: it provides a terminology for the description of empirical cases and the formulation of classifications and hypotheses. Weber writes:[6]

> . . . sociological analysis both abstracts from reality and at the same time helps us to understand it, in that it shows with what degree of approximation a concrete historical phenomenon can be subsumed under one or more of these concepts. For example,

the same historical phenomenon may be in one aspect feudal, in another patrimonial, in another bureaucratic, and in still another charismatic.

The ideal-type functions as a reference point which highlights aspects of concrete individual cases: for example how in certain respects an individual's opinions deviate from the ideal-type of Neo-liberal ideology. In addition, the ideal type facilitates comparison with other individual cases or other ideal-types. Third, in using the word 'ideal', Weber refers not to an ethical or normative perfection but instead to the complete logical integration (logical purity) which is characteristic of an ideal-type: that is, the elements of any 'ideal-type' form a logically consistent whole. Logical perfection distinguishes the ideal-type from reality because reality is often impure, that is, it mixes up elements which are (logically but not empirically) inconsistent.

In this study, ideal-types were used at two stages of the research process. First, they provided a theoretical justification of the interview topics and questions. Second, they guided analysis of data about the socio-political views of interviewees. Interviews generated evidence about opinions on particular issues and such evidence has to be transformed into evidence about the ideological orientations of interviewees. The transformation was achieved by using ideal-types.

3 CONSTRUCTING A TYPOLOGY OF CITY IDEOLOGIES

A typology of four ideal-typical ideologies was constructed in order to classify interviewees by ideology on the basis of interview data about their socio-political opinions. The ideal-typical ideologies were: (a) Neo-liberalism; (b) Traditional Conservatism; (c) Liberal Democracy; and (d) Democratic Socialism. These ideologies were chosen because each had influenced some of the interviewees. An ideal-type of Marxism was not constructed because none of the interviewees was in any respect whatsoever Marxist.

The construction of the typology of ideal-typical ideologies was a lengthy process. A paper on ideal-typical ideologies was written in the very early weeks of the interviews in an attempt to justify the ideal-types theoretically and to make sense of the answers provided to questions about privatisation and income tax in particular and in anticipation of the final analysis of interview data. To a large extent, the ideas incorporated in the typology pre-date the fieldwork even though they were only formulated explicitly and systematically once fieldwork had commenced. Particular authors – all are discussed below – were of enormous assistance in the sharpening up of early ideas. The authors all adhered, usually explicitly, to a particular ideological position and often characterised this in some detail. Furthermore, proponents of each ideology criticised writers with different ideological standpoints. The fact that proponents of ideologies both presented their own views and criticised those of others with different ideologies made it easier to pinpoint the overlaps and disagreements in the relationships of ideologies. Finally, reference was made to a range of other works which included systematic analyses of ideologies.[7]

As explained earlier, the construction of ideal-types always involves selection of features relevant to the research in question: the construction of the ideal-type here was consequently determined by the focus of this research on the relationship between the state and the market. Accordingly, many beliefs normally associated in everyday life with particular ideologies were not included in the ideal-typical ideologies because they are not pertinent. For example, the association of Neo-liberal views about the economy with traditional conceptions of order, family and morality in the phenomenon of the 'new right', is not relevant for present purposes.

The collection of interview data about socio-political opinions and the subsequent assignment of individuals to specific ideologies depends upon the existence of a means – initially unformulated and later systematic – of classification. The typology of ideal-types constitutes a system of classification or tool of analysis: it provides a systematic formulation of the key elements of each ideology and of the differences between the ideologies. It should be noted, however, that because there is some overlap between beliefs characteristic of different ideal-typical ideologies, allocation of interviewees to ideal-typical ideologies is often plagued by difficulties – this problem will be discussed in section 4.

The outline of the major features of each ideal-typical ideology is split into three sections dealing respectively with:

(a) how proponents of the ideology view the market;
(b) what overall roles, including economic roles, are assigned to the state;
(c) how the advocates of the ideology think we can most effectively maximise the freedoms enjoyed by those who live in the society.

The first two issues are central to this study. The third (the conditions of freedom) has been included because we can only understand views about the market and the state in the context of conceptions of what constitutes a free society. The researcher expected many interviewees to introduce the concept of freedom in response to questions about the role of the state in general and in relation to the market but, in fact, such references were infrequent.

In constructing the ideal-types, the work of certain authors was used both because each seemed to express the key elements of one or other of the ideological traditions mentioned above (Neo-liberalism, Traditional Conservatism, Liberal Democracy, Democratic Socialism) and because each criticised rival traditions in a manner which highlighted the differences between traditions. It must be emphasised at this point that the ideal-types are not summaries of the views of the authors; indeed, since the authors are individuals there are bound to be differences, both of substance and emphasis, between them.

The following writers[8] have been treated as more or less representative of the four ideal-typical ideologies:

(a) Neo-liberalism – Milton Friedman and Friedrich Hayek;
(b) Traditional Conservatism – Ian Gilmour and Francis Pym;
(c) Liberal Democracy – Shirley Williams, C. A. R. Crosland and David Owen[9];
(d) Democratic Socialism – Bernard Crick, Raymond Plant, Alec Nove, Geoff Hodgson, a group of Fabian writers about social security and R. H. Tawney.

(a) Neo-Liberalism

Neo-liberalism is characterised by the following beliefs[10]:
(i) The market economy maximises both economic efficiency and the freedom of choice of individuals.[11]

For Neo-liberals, the market is efficient because it is competitive. Firms and individuals are compelled to be efficient by cutting costs and innovating to win business. Firms and individuals have to respond to consumer preferences if they wish to sell their products or services. Furthermore, the market allows individuals to choose what work they do and what they wish to consume. In other words, the market enhances the prospects for individual freedom.

(ii) The state should be confined to strictly limited roles (the minimal state).[12]

Neo-liberals condemn state intervention in economic and social life, beyond a stringent minimum, because it undermines the competitive market by introducing regulation, subsidy and monopoly and destroys the basis for individual choice. The state should be confined to a few roles: the maintenance of law and order; defence against potential attack from outside the country; provision of a sound currency; action to secure the conditions for free competition; policy to guarantee a beneficial environment for business activity in a market free as far as possible of state regulation and state ownership. Only a basic level of social security can be justified and this only for those genuinely without the means to support themselves – such support should not undermine the incentives on which the market relies. The state should not run a wide-ranging welfare state and it should not pursue egalitarian aims.[13] State intervention in welfare substitutes coercion and compulsory taxation for free choice about spending priorities.

(iii) Freedom of the individual is the fundamental value.[14]

Neo-liberalism is concerned with the individual and the conditions of individual freedom. Freedom is conceived in terms of absence of constraints. State intervention (or what Neo-liberals term 'collectivism') often directly attacks individual freedom by restraining or removing free choice. 'Collectivism' is a threat to individual choice because it involves high compulsory taxation and because it substitutes state decisions for individual decisions on spending. State intervention also indirectly attacks individual freedom because it undermines the competitive market economy; the market economy is a precondition for freedom because it disperses power while state intervention concentrates power. They reject so-called 'positive freedoms' (for example, the rights to employment, to health care) because these involve collectivist social policy.

(b) Traditional Conservatism

Traditional Conservatism is characterised by the following beliefs[15]:
(i) Market solutions are preferred when they are viable.[16]
Gilmour summarises the positive view of the market very effectively[17]:

> He [the Traditional Conservative] prefers the market . . . for both political and economic reasons. It is decentralized and pluralistic. It operates by consent not coercion. . . . It is much more efficient.

However, when the market fails, state intervention is legitimate[18] and, indeed, obligatory.
(ii) The state is the guardian of the community.[19]
Traditional Conservatives wish to achieve a balance between the freedom of the individual and the interests of the community as a whole.[20] Societies are not just collections of individuals and the state is responsible for harmony between individual and community.

Traditional Conservatives prefer to rely on the market wherever possible and believe that state intervention undermines the competition which is an essential spur to efficiency. They maintain that the growth since 1945 of state intervention in economic and social policy (and the associated taxation) has been excessive and they wish to see state intervention cut back sharply[21]:

> There has been too much government meddling, and too much of it has been incompetent.

However, for Traditional Conservatives, the market is not sacrosanct. When the market fails the state must become involved.[22] For example, there is an economic role for the state in supporting important industries which are in crisis. Furthermore, the market is irrelevant to certain problems: it cannot protect the framework of the society because it only takes account of individual choices. The state must act in support of the cohesion and stability of the community where this proves necessary even if this involves interference with the market.[23]

The weak and the needy have a right to a decent level of community support through the welfare state. The state should not be confined to an absolutely minimal role. Considerations of humanity and social peace dictate that the state should act to contain and supplement the market when necessary. However, Traditional Conservatives reject egalitarian social policy[24] on the grounds that it is inimical to individual freedom and diversity and that it undermines the incentives which are crucial to a successful economy.

(iii) Traditional Conservatives seek a balance between the freedom of the individual and the well-being of the community and between the market and the state.[25]

Traditional Conservatives argue that a free society must be based upon a synthesis of the rights of individuals and the interests of the whole community (Nation). Individual freedom must be exercised within a framework acceptable to the community as a whole.

A free society can only exist on the basis of a market economy but the continuance of the market is dependent upon its legitimacy. The market will only be viewed as legitimate if the state acts to control its negative features and to protect the weak. Individual freedom requires a judicious mix of market processes and state intervention.

It should be clear by now that there are considerable differences between Neo-liberals and Traditional Conservatives on the issue of the legitimacy of state intervention in the market. However, one must not lose sight of the area of agreement. Adherents of both ideologies would support the four principles outlined in 1979 by the Chancellor of the Exchequer in his statement of the new Conservative government's aims.[26] Only the first three principles are relevant here: the need to 'strengthen incentives', 'enlarge freedom of choice for the individual' and reduce the 'burden of financing the public sector'.

(c) Liberal Democracy

Liberal Democracy is characterised by the following beliefs[27]:

(i) Liberal Democrats are enthusiastic about the market but believe that state intervention in the market is frequently necessary.[28]

Liberal Democrats believe that the market is normally efficient because it is competitive and cost-cutting and innovation results from competition. However, like the Traditional Conservative

but to a greater extent, they contend that a mix of state
intervention and market processes is inevitable and desirable.
They also favour the market because they believe it is a
prerequisite for individual choice. Finally, they fear
concentrations of power and believe that the market diffuses
power more widely than alternatives.

(ii) Liberal Democrats believe that the market cannot meet
certain economic and social needs. In such cases, state
intervention is appropriate but care should be taken to
decentralise such intervention.[29]

Liberal Democrats believe that state intervention in the
economy is frequently necessary. The state needs to act where the
market produces gross regional imbalances, where competition is
absent or weak, when important industries are under threat.
Similarly, the market is frequently the most efficient system
available but, sometimes, other means to meet human needs are
relevant or even preferable (for example, housing co-operatives).
Furthermore, where the market is irrelevant – where the common
needs of a community are concerned (environmental protection,
for example) – then the state should act because the market is only
the best option when individual choice is the issue.

Liberal Democrats are strongly committed to the welfare state
for three reasons. First, they believe that collective provision,
through the state, for the needy is essential. Second, they wish to
use social policy to reduce the inequality market processes
produce. Third, they fear the disunity and conflict which they
contend will always result from untrammelled market forces.

(iii) The Liberal Democrat pursues twin goals: maximum
individual freedom and a less unequal society but gives priority to
the former goal.[30]

Liberal Democrats believe that the freedom of individuals to
live as they choose is fundamental but substantial inequality
offends the Liberal Democrat. However, they eschew aggressive
egalitarian strategies which are thought to undermine individual
freedom; if they have to choose between the two goals of individual
freedom and less inequality, they will always prefer the first.

Liberal Democrats prefer market solutions when they are
feasible because they are thought to provide the basis for
individual choice and because markets fragment power and
diffused power is a precondition for individual freedom and civil
liberties.

(d) Democratic Socialism

The Democratic Socialist ideology is characterised by the following beliefs[31]:

(i) The Democratic Socialist wishes to reconcile the market and planning to achieve both economic growth and the equitable distribution of the fruits of such growth.[32]

Democratic Socialists are suspicious of the market but recognise that it is an inevitable and, to the extent that it is efficient, a desirable feature of economic life. Market forces should not be allowed free reign: the market is thought to develop in a haphazard manner in response to opportunities for private profit rather than in relation to social needs. The ideal is a society where the sphere of the market and private ownership of giant companies is diminishing and planning and public and co-operative forms of ownership and organisation are becoming more significant.

(ii) State intervention is necessary to protect the interests of the community as a whole and to correct negative consequences of market processes.[33]

Democratic Socialists strongly support collective provision for basic needs (both social and individual) and state intervention to remedy the defects of the market. In a democratic society, such initiatives are the only means available to counteract the powerful wealthy minorities and organisations which dominate the economy; furthermore, state intervention makes possible an attention to matters other than the logic of profitability. Finally, the welfare state is viewed as a means both to soften the insecurities of life, especially for the disadvantaged, and to achieve greater equality. Greater equality is thought to be a good in itself and to increase efficiency because it raises morale and commitment amongst subordinate groups.[34]

(iii) The Democratic Socialist believes that liberty and equality are inextricably intertwined. These values can only be realised if those who wield power are accountable to the community.[35]

Democratic Socialists believe that individuals cannot really be free if they lack the means to exercise formal rights. Greater equality will make these rights a reality for all. However, equality without liberty is a nightmare. State intervention must take place in a framework which guarantees and supports such liberty.

Democratic Socialists are concerned also about inequalities of power and how these constrain the freedom of the many. The uncontrolled market allows giant corporations and the wealthy enormous power. State intervention to reduce the concentration of power and to democratise organisational structures is thought necessary.

4   ALLOCATION OF INTERVIEWEES TO IDEOLOGIES

Each ideal-typical ideology is associated with particular views about the interview topics (privatisation, progressive income taxation, unemployment). Views on interview topics can, therefore, be treated as indicators of ideological orientation. Consequently, data about the socio-political views of interviewees are used to classify interviewees in terms of ideologies. Data used includes, in addition to views on the topics just mentioned, each interviewee's answer to a question about what industries (if any) the state should own. Section 4 is divided into four parts which examine respectively:

(a) the views on interview topics associated with each ideal-typical ideology;

(b) problems encountered when allocating interviewees to ideologies;

(c) the results of the allocation by ideology;

(d) the relationship between age and ideological orientation.

(a) Ideologies and socio-political views

How are the views expressed in interviews associated with each ideology? In the introduction to chapter 2, the way in which the interview topics (privatisation, income tax, unemployment) reflect interviewees' views on the desirable relationship between state and market was explained. Views about privatisation reflect the individual's conception of the proper relationship between the market and the state: consequently, such views can be used as an indicator of the ideological orientation of the individual. Neo-liberals favour the privatisation programme without reservation on efficiency and competition grounds. Furthermore, for the Neo-liberal, all privatisation is a tremendous blow against state intervention in the market and against collectivism. On the privatisation of BT (British Telecom), Neo-liberals are wholly favourable despite, in a few cases, a worry about BT being a monopoly.

Traditional Conservatives on the whole favour privatisation because they are pro-market but express doubts about proceeding on the basis of general principles rather than taking the individual circumstances of industries into account. Traditional Conservatives favour the privatisation of BT on efficiency and competition grounds but often with some reservations (for example, BT a monopoly, BT a state asset).

Liberal Democrats believe that the type of ownership of a firm or industry is in itself unimportant: what matters is whether the industry or firm is satisfactorily run from the point of view of consumers and the community. Some privatisation is supported but on a case-by-case basis; they dislike the 'doctrinaire' assumption of a systematic privatisation policy that private ownership is always preferable. On the sale of BT, Liberal Democrats will express 'mixed views' for two reasons. First, the essential feature of this ideology is an empirical or pragmatic orientation which often results in tentative judgements about, for example, the argument that privatisation of BT has increased competition and efficiency. Second, they are, despite being pragmatists, also supporters of the general principle of a 'mixed economy' and this makes it difficult for them to come down clearly on one side or other.

Democratic Socialists strongly support public ownership and oppose all attempts to sell off state assets. They believe that the state should own 'basic' industries (for example, transport, power) and some of the giant corporations, these latter being seen as great centres of power. They oppose the privatisation of BT because it is the sale of a major national asset and has resulted in the loss of control over a crucial and powerful industry.

An individual's view about progressive income taxation reflects two aspects of his or her ideological orientation: first, the attitude towards the legitimacy of attempts by the state to alter the distributional outcomes of market processes; second, the attitude towards equality and inequality. Both aspects are central features of the ideal-typical ideologies. Progressive income taxation is the crucial issue which divides Neo-liberals from the other three ideologies: Neo-liberals oppose progressive income taxation because it is an attempt to interfere with market outcomes. All the other ideologies support progressive income taxation but in varying degrees and with different goals in mind. Traditional Conservatives think that it is 'fair' that the poor be helped in this way but the pursuit of equality is vigorously rejected. Liberal Democrats support progressive income taxation because they support a mild degree of egalitarian redistribution. Democratic Socialists support a heavily graduated system of progressive income taxation in order to achieve a substantial redistribution of income.

Views about the state's role in dealing with unemployment provide a good indicator of ideology because they reflect interviewees' views of the proper relationship between the state and the market. Only Neo-liberals oppose higher state expenditure as a means to decrease unemployment. The other three groups favour reflation, using higher levels of state spending, but in varying degrees. Traditional Conservatives and Liberal Democrats regard reflation as a supplement to the market. Democratic Socialists are more sceptical of the market's potential than are both Traditional Conservatives and Liberal Democrats and favour an even greater role for state intervention – a larger increase in state expenditure and a wider range of initiatives by public sector bodies.

Key points about the ideal-typical ideologies and the socio-political views associated with each are summarised in two tables. Table 5.1 summarises the position of the four ideal-typical ideologies (Neo-liberalism, Traditional Conservatism, Liberal Democracy, Democratic Socialism) on certain fundamental issues about the relationship between the market and the state. Table 5.2 summarises the position of each ideal-typical ideology on the interview topics. It should be noted that individual judgement is an intrinsic feature of the construction of ideal-types: the foregoing discussion and Tables 5.1 and 5.2 inevitably reflect that of the researcher.

(b) Problems encountered when allocating by ideology

Three problems arose during the analysis of data for the purpose of allocation by ideology. First, and this is the easiest of the problems, seven individuals were not classified. In six cases this was a result of insufficient information: for example, one merchant banker stated that she thought the privatisation policy was 'wonderful' but it was not possible to ask her about other

TABLE 5.1　*Key tenets of each ideal-typical ideology*

	Ideal-typical ideology			
Issue	Neo-liberalism	Traditional Conservative	Liberal Democracy	Democratic Socialism
Egalitarian	No	No	Mildly	Strongly
Trusts in the market alone?	Yes	Yes, when it works. Otherwise, state must intervene.	Market usually most efficient but be pragmatic: co-ops and the like valuable.	No, market often fails and state intervention often needed.
State's role				
general	Anti-intervention.	State as guardian.	Significant role for state.	Strongly interventionist.
in economy	Minimal: value of money, competition and so on.	To intervene when market fails or is irrelevant.	To intervene when market fails or is irrelevant.	Positive role: control or replace market if necessary. Should own crucial industries.
in social policy	Dismantle welfare state.	Welfare state valuable but trim.	Defend welfare state: use for mild redistribution.	Strengthen welfare state: egalitarian aims.

socio-political issues. In the seventh case, a young woman jobber, the replies were confused or incoherent: her views on specific topics being unclear, she could not be classified by ideology.

Second, most individuals do not exemplify one of the (pure) ideal-types: their views draw on elements of more than one ideal-typical ideology. Such interviewees were often very difficult to classify. For example, a director of a merchant bank[36] opposes progressive income tax, supports privatisation without reservation, sees no role whatsoever for state ownership (including the NHS) – until this point, he is a pure Neo-liberal. On the topic of unemployment, he stated that the government's market-based strategy has failed, and he would support a complete reversal. On being pressed to elucidate, he became

TABLE 5.2   *Views of each ideal-typical ideology on interview topics*

| Interview topic | Ideal-typical ideology | | | |
	Neo-liberalism	Traditional Conservative	Liberal Democracy	Democratic Socialism
Privatisation of BT	Favours strongly	Favours, possibly with reservations	'Mixed' views	Opposes strongly.
Privatisation in general	Favours strongly	Favours with some reservations.	Doubtful	Opposes strongly
Progressive Income Tax	Opposes	Favours: help 'poor' and/or pragmatic grounds.	Favours: mildly egalitarian.	Favours strongly: egalitarian.
Is government doing enough about unemploy-ment?	Yes.	No.	No.	No.
What policies advocated?	Leave market to cope. Supply-side measures. Cut state spending. De-regulate industry.	Encourage-ment of market not sufficient. Increase state spending. Don't make a fetish of market.	Reflate: increase state spending. Market and state intervention both essential.	Reflate: large increase in state spending. Intervention-ist strategy.

irritable and finally asserted that something 'has' to be done but that he is not an economist and does not know what can or should be done. His position on unemployment is not that of a Neo-liberal but that of a Traditional Conservative. He was classified 'between Neo-liberalism and Traditional Conservatism'.

The third problem is endemic to interpretive sociology which deals with what people say, that is, with meanings. Meanings are notoriously difficult to classify because they are not amenable to exact measurement unless one is prepared to sacrifice qualitative richness in the search for a spurious precision. Quite simply, the criteria for allocation to ideal-typical ideologies summarised in Table 5.2 cannot be precisely and mechanically applied. Answers to questions were examined against the pre-formulated criteria for allocation to ideal-types but, because meanings cannot be precisely measured and qualifications cannot be weighted in an exact manner, ultimately, classification is a matter of judgement. For example, how should one interpret 'I support progressive income tax as long as the top rates are not disincentives to enterprise'? In each case interpretation was a matter of balancing conformity with, or discrepancy from, the features of each ideal type against an overall impression of the individual's outlook. On occasions, essential information was lacking or replies were incoherent. Incidentally, the view that precise classification can be achieved by assigning points to answers using a pre-formulated scale and deciding on the position where one ideology ends and another begins, neglects the fact that the points would be based on criteria which are ultimately just as arbitrary as the judgements made here.

The difficulties associated with interpretation and allocation were most noticeable when scrutinising answers to the question about what industries the state should run: except for Neo-liberals, the individual usually responds with a list (for example, gas, NHS, and so on) or a term (for instance, 'basic industries'); there is no straightforward method for determining the borderline between, say, a Traditional Conservative view of industry and someone who stands 'between Neo-liberalism and Traditional Conservatism'. Furthermore, often individuals make statements which do not hang together in an unambiguously consistent whole and this makes the difficulties of allocation even more intractable. The qualifications outlined in this paragraph must be borne in mind when considering the data presented in Tables 5.3 and 5.4 below. The validity of the allocation to ideologies is based upon the fact that classification of each individual to an ideology can be rationally defended by reference to data about the individual's views and the pre-formulated criteria of allocation. In the final analysis, however, assignment to ideologies has inevitably been a matter of judgement.

(c) Allocation to ideologies

Ideal-types are characterised by logical consistency. Many interviewees, of course, diverge from this 'ideal' of logical consistency and cannot be allocated to one of the ideal-typical ideologies. Such individuals have been placed in one or other of the categories between the ideal-types: such categorisation provides information about the ideologies of the many individuals who could not be allocated to one of the ideal-typical ideologies. The necessity of categories such as 'between Neo-liberalism and Traditional Conservatism' (Table 5.3) follows from the fact that every individual has an ideology (or ideological orientation) but only some concrete ideologies can be considered as exemplifications of the ideal-typical ideologies discussed earlier in this chapter.

Given that most individuals could not be classified under one or other ideal-type, how can the value of the typology be defended? The answer is (as explained in section 2) that the ideal-type is an analytic tool of comparison. The ideal-types are an explicit formulation of the relevant key elements of each ideology: they function as reference points which highlight significant aspects of the socio-political views of individuals and allow us to compare individuals with the ideal-types and with each other in a systematic fashion. They also enable us to classify individuals by ideology on the basis of their views and the features included in each ideal-type.

Table 5.3 summarises the results of the allocation of interviewees to ideologies.

TABLE 5.3   *Classification of sample by ideology*

Classification	Percentage of individuals who were classified
Ideal-typical Neo-liberal	7%
between Neo-Liberalism and Traditional Conservatism	46%
Ideal-typical Traditional Conservative	33%
between Traditional Conservatism and Liberal Democracy	5%
Ideal-typical Liberal Democrat	4%
between Liberal Democracy and Democratic Socialism	1%
Ideal-typical Democratic Socialist	3%
Total number of individuals classified	91
Individuals not classified	7
Total interviewees	98

Table 5.3 shows that those classified as Neo-liberals or Traditional Conservatives and those categorised as being 'between Neo-liberalism and Traditional Conservatism' together constitute 78 (86 per cent) of the 91 interviewees who could be classified. These interviewees favour a severe curtailment of the state's role in the economy and in social policy: that is, all these individuals favour the privatisation and taxation policies of the post-1979 Conservative administrations. These interviewees are very pro-market indeed. However, only Neo-liberals and those categorised as standing 'between Neo-liberalism and Traditional Conservatism' reject the fundamental institutional elements of the post-war consensus in favour of a complete or virtually complete market society: these two groups together constitute 48 (53 per cent) out of 91 individuals classified. Only 13 (14 per cent) out of 91 interviewees oppose, although to varying degrees (see below) the main drift of the Thatcher government's socio-economic policies: these are the only interviewees who manifested an inclination to protect some, although not usually all, of the fundamental features of the post-war consensus. The data in Table 5.3 (taken together with the evidence in chapter 2 comparing interviewees' socio-political views with those of the wider British population), support Spiegelberg's statement (quoted at the head of this chapter) that:

> The more pure and limited capitalist viewpoint is at its most trenchant and pervasive in the City.

(d) Relationship between age and ideology

In chapter 4, the relationship between pro-market views and age was examined in order to demonstrate that City recruits were strongly pro-market before entry to trainee posts. The data on ideological orientations of interviewees summarised in Table 5.3 provide another opportunity to analyse the relationship between age and socio-political views, in this case these views are indicated by ideological orientation. Table 5.4 summarises the breakdown by age of the data on ideologies of interviewees. It must be emphasised that the allocation to ideologies is based to a large extent on socio-political views as indicated by answers to questions on privatisation, progressive income taxation and unemployment. Therefore, data on the ideologies of interviewees

TABLE 5.4   *Relationship between ideology and age*

| | Percentage of individuals in each group | | | | |
Classification	All interviewees	20–29	30–39	40–49	50+
Neo-liberal	7%	4%	17%	4%	0%
between Neo-liberal and Traditional Conservative	46%	50%	29%	52%	57%
Traditional Conservative	33%	29%	29%	40%	36%
between Traditional Conservative and Liberal Democrat	5%	7%	4%	4%	7%
Liberal Democrat	4%	4%	13%	0%	0%
between Liberal Democrat and Democratic Socialist	1%	0%	4%	0%	0%
Democratic Socialist	3%	7%	4%	0%	0%
Total individuals classified	91	28	24	25	14
Total individuals not classified	7	2	3	2	0
Totals	98	30	27	27	14

broken down by age are not independent of the data presented in Tables 4.1 (views on progressive income tax broken down by age) and 4.2 (views about privatisation broken down by age). However, Table 5.4 allows us to see whether the youngest age group are appreciably less influenced by Neo-liberalism than the older age groups. If this were the case, Table 5.4 would lead to conclusions rather different from those in chapter 4 where younger interviewees (those aged 20 to 29) were seen to be almost as strongly pro-market as older interviewees (those aged 30 and over).

Table 5.4 shows that for those individuals who were classified by ideology: in all age groups around 50 per cent are classified as Neo-liberals or stand 'between Neo-liberalism and Traditional Conservatism'. Such individuals were all heavily influenced by Neo-liberalism or, to put it differently, rejected the institutions of the post-1945 political settlement. Percentages are: for all classified, 53 per cent; for those 20–29, 54 per cent; 30–39, 46 per cent; 40–49, 56 per cent; 50+, 57 per cent. These figures suggest that roughly the same proportion of younger interviewees (under 30) are strongly pro-market as is the case for older interviewees (those over 30).

Individuals classified as 'between Traditional Conservatism and Liberal Democracy', Liberal Democrat, 'between Liberal Democracy and Democratic Socialism', and Democratic Socialist all defended the post-1945 political settlement, although to varying degrees. Traditional Conservatives were excluded from this category of defenders of the post-1945 settlement because they strongly supported virtually every specific privatisation and many of them were happy with the serious weakening of the system of progressive income taxation since 1979. If the defenders of the post-1945 settlement (Traditional Conservatives being excluded) are added together they constitute 14 per cent of all interviewees who were classified by ideology; of those 20–29, 18 per cent; 30–39, 25 per cent; 40–49, 4 per cent; 50+, 4 per cent.

The analysis above indicates that the 30–39 group is the most favourable to the institutions of the post-1945 consensus: it has the lowest percentage of those wishing to dismantle the institutions of the post-1945 settlement and the highest percentage inclined to defend them. Of the other age groups, only the 20–29 contains a significant complement of individuals willing to defend the institutions of the consensus although such individuals are swamped by those who are strongly pro-market.

Overall, figures in Table 5.4 suggest (as did the data in chapter 4) that young interviewees are very pro-market. They are less pro-market than interviewees aged 40 and over but surprisingly more pro-market than those aged 30–39. Perhaps the ideological difference between the two youngest age groups is explained by the change in the wider ideological and political context in British society in the last decade or so.[37]

5 CASE-STUDIES

This section provides a number of illustrative case-studies taken from the interviews.

(a) A Neo-liberal

A stockbroker,[38] when asked what industries the state should own and run, rejected any role whatsoever for state ownership of industry:

Stockbroker:	'I don't see that they need to own and run any. The sooner British Rail is privatised, the sooner British Airways is privatised, the sooner the steel companies are privatised, the better – as far as I can see.'
Interviewer:	'So, this would include things like Thames Water?'
Stockbroker:	'Absolutely.'
Interviewer:	'. . . What about the National Health Service? . . . Would you privatise it?'
Stockbroker:	'Why not?'
Interviewer:	'For everyone?'
Stockbroker:	'Mm.'

Furthermore, he opposed a system of progressive income taxation because market rewards reflect hard work and progressive income taxation destroys this relationship:

> I think there ought to be a maximum that any one person pays in any one year in terms of income tax. And, if you are able to earn more than a fixed amount, well then 'Jolly good luck to you!' because you're obviously working extraordinarily hard. Nobody just hands out money.

(b) Two individuals 'between Neo-liberalism and Traditional Conservatism'

A young market-maker in the traded options market[39] saw no role for state ownership other than of the NHS but was quite happy to support progressive taxation (which alters market outcomes) so long as the higher rates were not so high that they destroyed incentives – in his opinion, one pays a lot of tax only if one has a very high income.

A senior jobber[40] opposed state ownership except for the water industry (because he believed that a private water industry would not respect fundamental ecological considerations) and British Rail (it is essential but unprofitable). He strongly supported progressive income taxation and roundly criticised the first budget of the new Conservative administration in 1979 for lowering top tax rates 'when she gave to those that have more than they needed'.

Both these individuals are strong supporters of market provision but are prepared to support progressive income taxation because they believe that the poorest need protecting by the community.

(c) A Traditional Conservative

This very senior banker[41] supports the privatisation policy on the whole but contends that some state ownership, on social and strategic grounds, is necessary. The state needs to play a role in industries which are essential to the country: consequently, although he favours the privatisation of BT, the state 'needs to keep a hand on the tiller'; the state should own the steel industry, one or two shipyards, naval shipyards and Royal Ordnance; the National Health Service should not be privatised although some services within it (for example, laundry) should be. He believes that the state has definite responsibilities with respect to the development of the economy:

> Whatever one says about modernising industry . . . and making industry more competitive in the world, the government has a social duty to ensure that this country changes in as an acceptable way as possible to the population. You cannot just close down whole sectors of British industry and expect the population to sit there and just accept it. . . . I believe that governments do have a duty to ensure that their people are looked after in as best way they can.

(d) Individual 'between Traditional Conservatism and Liberal Democracy'

This merchant banker[42] sees no particular virtue in the privatisation policy. He takes a pragmatic view: activities of a commercial nature are more appropriately situated in the private sector (Amersham International, British Aerospace). In other cases (public utilities like Gas), a private monopoly will be no more efficient than a state firm. BT is on the margin: to the extent that it will compete internationally, there is a virtue in privatisation. The NHS should remain much as it is although some activities at the margin could be privatised:

No, I think the basic public nature of health care in this country is something which should be maintained.

He favours progressive income taxation: he does not believe that market incomes 'purely' reflect hard work and ability: those who believe they do, do not follow their argument to its logical conclusion, which is that everyone should start equal, which would make for 'an uncomfortable society'. There are, he continued, bound to be inequalities in economic performance and the community should make an effort to introduce 'some equalisation'. He also criticised the government's unwillingness to increase expenditure to reduce unemployment, referring to 'an unreasoned fear of government expenditure'.

(e) A Liberal Democrat

This young merchant banker[43] said that the Conservative government has privatised because it has committed itself to reducing the Public Sector Borrowing Requirement (PSBR) and has needed cash to achieve this aim. The government claims that privatisation will increase competition but, in fact, it has impeded competition: for example, British Airways (BA) had been favoured in route-allocations by the government as against the privately-owned British Caledonian in order to push up the price at which BA could be sold – as a result, competition has suffered. Similarly, BT (British Telecom) was privatised as a monopoly because of the government's short-term need for cash to meet its PSBR targets: it would have been far better to keep BT under state ownership and subject it to real competition. To her, competition and not the ownership of an industry is the crucial issue: why should one expect a privatised monopoly to be more efficient or charge lower prices? She said that she is not 'anti-private ownership *per se*' and she does believe that the direct involvement of the state in industry should be 'marginally reduced' partly because the government tends to constantly interfere with nationalised industries and disrupt their progress. However, efficiency should not be the 'only yardstick': firms have been nationalised for 'a reason' (for example, on social control grounds); this means that there are grounds for state ownership even if pure market efficiency suffers. She stated that she thinks that City salaries are too high and she favours progressive income taxation:

Well, it seems to me to be completely just and it seems to me to be the only practical way of raising money because if you tax the rich less you'd have to tax the poor more and they can't afford it.

She was asked how she felt about altering the pattern of rewards which came out of the market and she replied:

Well, I'm not quite as enamoured of the market system as Milton Friedman is . . . .

(f) Individual 'between Liberal Democracy and Democratic Socialism'

This senior fund manager[44] was the only strong egalitarian in the sample: he refused to accept that anyone should earn ten times what others earn or own two houses when some people do not own even one. He referred frequently to the need to redistribute income and wealth and stressed his commitment to an equal society where everyone received the same amount of income; he supports progressive income taxation as a means to that goal. His egalitarianism is stronger than that normally associated with the ideal-typical Democratic Socialist. Yet, he regarded the type of ownership of industry as an irrelevance: what matters is not who owns industry but that it is efficiently run; the fruits of industry should then be equally distributed. On one count (strong egalitarianism) he is a Democratic Socialist but on another (irrelevance of the private ownership/public ownership distinction) he is a Liberal Democrat: therefore, he was not allocated to either ideal-type but was classified as 'between Liberal Democracy and Democratic Socialism'.

(g) A Democratic Socialist

This stockbroker,[45] whose father was a manual worker and strong trade unionist (mother: housewife), criticised the sale of BT:

No, I'm strongly opposed to it . . . I think it's disgusting that a nationalised asset can be . . . sold off like this to just line people's pockets, which is all it has done because it has no economic merits at all – absolutely none.

He vigorously opposed the overall privatisation programme:

No, I'm against it all. There's no . . . all it is is really dismantling the social fabric which has been built up steadily since the War.

On progressive income taxation, he stated that he is 'completely happy' with it and, when asked 'Why?', he stated:

> I think it . . . it just has to be fair if you believe in a Socialist world . . . it's, I mean, taking from the rich to give to, I mean, in theory the people that haven't got as much money. So I can't see how anyone dare complain about that at all.

6   SUMMARY

When interviewees are classified by ideology, it is clear that they are, in all but a small minority of cases, heavily influenced by Neo-liberal ideology. When we take account of the fact that the Traditional Conservative ideal-type is associated with the acceptance of the bulk of the privatisation programme and a severely weakened progressive income taxation system, it is clear that only a small minority of interviewees defend the post-1945 settlement and then often (for example, those classified 'between Traditional Conservatism and Liberal Democracy', Liberal Democrat, 'between Liberal Democracy and Democratic Socialism') only certain of its aspects. A breakdown of interviewees' ideologies by age demonstrated a strong pro-market tendency among the youngest age group. Surprisingly, those in the next age group (30–39) were less pro-market than the youngest, perhaps, reflecting wider political changes since the 1970s.

These conclusions highlight the nature of the City consensus. Effectively, the City 'dissenter' is an individual who favours the social institutions of the post-War consensus, usually somewhat diluted. Although those who defend the post-1945 political settlement do question the principle of the absolute superiority of the market, the uncritical acceptance of the capitalist nature of the economy by such dissenters is striking. It is extraordinary that only one person even mentioned the possibility of being 'for' or 'against' capitalism (he is classified as 'between Liberal Democracy and Democratic Socialism').

NOTES

1. R. Spiegelberg, *The City*: p. 2.
2. References on ideology included: K. Mannheim, *Ideology and Utopia*: especially chapter 2; J. Plamenatz, *Ideology*: esp. chapter 1; K. Marx and F. Engels, *The German Ideology*: chapter 1, A (i.e., pp. 29–64); R. Williams, *Keywords*: pp. 126–30; R. Williams, *Marxism and Literature*: chapter 4; E. Shils, 'Ideology' in his *The Constitution of Society* (esp. pp. 202–4).
3. For useful critiques of pro-market (or 'Neo-liberal') ideologies, see: R. Plant, *Equality, Markets and the State*; G. Hodgson, *The Democratic Economy*: chapters 3, 4 and 6.
4. See: Weber, *Economy and Society*, i: 19–22 and his ' "Objectivity" in the Social Sciences' in Weber, *The Methodology of the Social Sciences* (esp. pp. 89–104).
5. Weber, ' "Objectivity" in the Social Sciences' in Weber, *The Methodology of the Social Sciences*: pp. 76–8.
6. Weber, *Economy and Society*, i: 20. See also *The Methodology of the Social Sciences*: p. 97.
7. The following references proved invaluable when the ideal-typical ideologies were being constructed: V. George and P. Wilding, *Ideology and Social Welfare*: chapters 2–5; D. Wedderburn, 'Theories of the Welfare State' in R. Miliband and J. Saville (eds), *Socialist Register, 1965*: especially, pp. 135–42; R. Mishra, *The Welfare State in Crisis*: chapters 2–5; N. Harris, *Beliefs in Society*: pp. 119–23.
8. See below for specific references.
9. The term 'Liberal Democracy' does not only include supporters of the (now defunct) British Liberal Party and British Social Democratic Party. The term refers to an ideology rather than to particular political parties.
10. This discussion of Neo-liberalism is based upon a study of the following: M. Friedman, *Capitalism and Freedom*: Introduction, chapters 1 and 2; M. Friedman and R. Friedman, *Free to Choose*: Introduction, chapters 1, 4 and 5 and 10; Hayek, *The Road to Serfdom*: chapters I, III, V–IX and XIV; Hayek, *The Constitution of Liberty*: chapters 1, 4–7, 9, 14, 17, 19, 20, 24; Hayek, *Law, Legislation, Liberty*: chapters 2, 9 and 10. See also: H. Spencer, *The Man Versus The State*: 'Six Essays on Government, Society, And Freedom'; J. S. Mill, *Principles of Political Economy*: chapter X1; R. Plant, *Equality, Markets and the State*: chapters 2–4; D. J. Manning, *Liberalism*: pp. 94–107.
11. See, for instance: Friedman, *Capitalism and Freedom*: chapter 1; Friedman and Friedman, *Free to Choose*: Introduction, chapters 1, 2 and 7; Hayek, *The Road to Serfdom*: chapters III and IV; Hayek, *Law, Legislation, Liberty*: chapter 10.
12. See: Friedman, *Capitalism and Freedom*: Introduction and chapter 2; Hayek, *The Road to Serfdom*: III – IX; Hayek, *The Constitution of Liberty:* chapters 6, 9, 17, 19, 20 and 24. See also H. Spencer, *The Man Versus the State*: 'Six Essays on Government, Society, and Freedom', Letter 1, especially p. 187.
13. Friedman and Friedman, *Free to Choose*: pp. 166–7. See also: Hayek, *Law, Legislation, Liberty*: chapter 9, especially p. 68.; Hayek, *The Road to Serfdom*: chapters III and VIII.

14.   See, for example: Friedman, *Capitalism and Freedom*: Introduction and chapter 1; Hayek, *The Road to Serfdom*: chapters I and III; Hayek, *The Constitution of Liberty*: chapters 1, 9 and 10; Hayek, *Law, Legislation, Liberty*: chapters 2 and 10.

15.   See: I. Gilmour, *Inside Right:* especially Part 1, chapter 1 and Part 3, chapters 1–3 and 6; I. Gilmour, *Britain Can Work*: especially chapters 1, 4, 6, 7 and 11; F. Pym, *The Politics of Consent*: chapters 1, 7, 8, 10 and 11.

16.   See: Gilmour, *Inside Right*: 'Post-War Conservatism' (especially, pp. 19–20), 'Conservative Philosophy' (especially, pp. 115–20) and 'The Economy'; Gilmour, *Britain Can Work*: especially, pp. 9–13 and 221.

17.   Gilmour, *Inside Right*: 'The Economy', p. 233.

18.   Gilmour, *Inside Right*: p. 235. See also: Gilmour, *Britain Can Work*: pp. 9–13 and 221.

19.   See: Gilmour, *Britain Can Work:* pp. 52–3 and pp., 168–70; Gilmour, *Inside Right*: 'Tory Themes', pp. 151–2; Pym, *The Politics of Consent*: chapters 7 and 8 and p. 174. See also: Samuel H. Beer, *Modern British Politics:* pp. 266–71 and 303–8.

20.   See, for instance: Gilmour, *Britain Can Work*: pp. 52, 156, 203 and 225; Gilmour, *Inside Right*: 'Conservative Philosophy' and 'Tory Themes'; Pym, *The Politics of Consent*: pp. 117–27.

21.   Gilmour, *Inside Right*: p. 236.

22.   Gilmour, *Britain Can Work*: p. 169.

23.   Gilmour, *Inside Right*: p. 118; Pym, *The Politics of Consent*: pp., 117–20.

24.   Gilmour, *Inside Right*: pp. 173–83.

25.   See: Gilmour, *Inside Right*: pp. 118 and 146–52; Gilmour, *Britain Can Work*: pp. 52, 179 and 203–4; Pym, *The Politics of Consent*: pp. 117–27 and chapter 11.

26.   P. Donaldson, *A Question of Economics*: p. 38.

27.   This discussion of Liberal Democracy draws mainly upon the following: S. Williams, *Politics is for People*; D. Owen, *A Future That Will Work*: chapters 1, 3, 7 and 8; D. Owen, *Face the Future*: chapters 1, 3, 6, 10 and 11; David Steel and Richard Holme (eds), *Partners in One Nation*: chapters 1, 2, 6, 7 and 10.

28.   See: S. Williams, *Politics is for People*: pp. 17–19 and 28–30; D. Owen, *A Future That Will Work*: chapter 1; D. Owen, *Face the Future*: chapters 1, 6 and 11; D. Steel and R. Holme (eds), *Partners in One Nation*: chapters 1 (Steel, 'Economic Recovery Through Partnership') and 2 (J. E. Meade, 'Full Employment, Wage Restraint, and the Distribution of Income'); 'Twelve tasks for Social Democrats' in Social Democratic Party, *Newsletter*, No., 1, April 1981.

29.   See: Williams, *Politics is for People*: pp. 28–32, 36–8 and chapter 10; Owen, *A Future That Will Work*: pp. 50–2 and chapter 7; Owen, *Face the Future*: chapters 1 and 3; Steel and Holme (eds), *Partners in One Nation*: pp. 30–3 (in papers by Meade – see note 28); 'Twelve tasks for Social Democrats' in Social Democratic Party, *Newsletter*, No. 1, April 1981.

30.   See: Williams, *Politics is for People*: pp. 28–30 and 204–6; D. Owen, *Face the Future*: chapters 1, 3 and 11; Steel and Holme (eds), *Partners in One Nation*: chapters 6 (R. Dahrendorf, 'The New Social State: a Liberal Perspective') and 7 (R. Holme, 'Political Accountability and the Exercise of Power').

31.   This discussion of Democratic Socialism is based to a large extent upon

the writings of R. H. Tawney: *The Acquisitive Society*: especially, chapter 7; *The Attack and Other Papers*: 'The Choice Before the Labour Party'; *Equality*: Prefaces, chapter 5 and 'Epilogue': section iii; *The Radical Tradition*: Part 3, chapters 8, 10 and 11. In addition, reference was made to more recent discussions. In particular: B. Crick, *Socialist Values and Time*; Fabian Society, *Social Security: The Real Agenda:* chapters 1 and 8; G. Hodgson, *The Democratic Economy: A new look at planning, markets and power*; A. Nove, *The Economics of Feasible Socialism*: Parts 4 and 5; M. Mann, *Socialism Can Survive: Social Change and the Labour Party*: chapters 7 and 9; R. Plant, *Equality, Markets and the State*.

32.   See: Tawney, *The Radical Tradition*: 'British Socialism Today' (paper originally published in 1952); Tawney, *Equality*: Prefaces, p. 30 (This is in the Preface to the 1938 edition) and 'Epilogue 1938–50', p. 230; Tawney, *The Attack and Other Papers*: 'The Choice Before the Labour Party', p. 69 (paper originally published 1934); Nove, *The Economics of Feasible Socialism*: pp. 154–76 and Part 5; Hodgson, *The Democratic Economy*: Parts 2 and 3.

33.   On state intervention in the economy, see: Tawney, *The Attack and Other Papers*: 'The Choice Before the Labour Party', p. 69; Tawney, *The Radical Tradition*: 'British Socialism Today', p. 183; Nove, *The Economics of Feasible Socialism*: Part 5; Hodgson, *The Democratic Economy*: chapters 10 and 11. On social policy, see: Crick, *Socialist Values and Time*: chapter 3; Plant, *Equality, Markets and the State*; Mann, *Socialism Can Survive;* chapter 9; Fabian Society, *Social Security: the Real Agenda*: chapters 1 and 8.

34.   Plant, *Equality, Markets and the State:* p. 23; Crick, *Socialist Values and Time*: p. 19; Hodgson, *The Democratic Economy*: chapter 9.

35.   On freedom, see: Tawney, *Equality*: pp. 164–73, 191–2 and 224–35; Tawney, *The Radical Tradition*: 'The Problem of the Public Schools' (especially p. 72), 'The Conditions of Economic Liberty' (pp. 106–13), 'Social Democracy in Britain' (pp. 165–73); Plant, *Equality, Markets and the State*; Crick, *Socialist Values and Time*: chapter 3. On democratisation of power, see: Tawney, *Equality*: pp. 191 and 230; Tawney, *The Radical Tradition*: 'The Conditions of Economic Liberty', pp. 106–15; Hodgson, *The Democratic Economy*: chapter 9.

36.   Taped interview: 202.

37.   To come to a firmer conclusion, we require longitudinal data: that is, data on the socio-political opinions of young people relative to older age groups over time. The writer was unable to find relevant material.

38.   Taped interview: 162.

39.   Taped interview: 198.

40.   Taped interview: 152.

41.   Taped interview: 155.

42.   Taped interview: 170.

43.   Taped interview: 145.

44.   Taped interview: 176.

45.   Taped interview: 174.

6 Markets, City Culture and Socialisation

1 INTRODUCTION

The issue of the origins of strongly pro-market views has been raised on a number of occasions. This chapter takes up this issue again in relation to the question of how recruits to City firms are socialised into a City culture which is characterised above all by its enthusiasm for markets and its ideological homogeneity.

The conclusions of the chapter are speculative. Future research is essential to establish whether the arguments developed are valid.

In previous chapters, the relative homogeneity of belief and ideology in the City has been emphasised. As explained in chapter 4, it is likely that recruits begin their City careers with exceptionally strong pro-market views. Work in the City financial markets subsequently both strengthens the pro-market assumptions held by individuals and silences doubts about whether it is appropriate to apply the market principle to all areas in which goods and services are produced and distributed. What are the mechanisms involved which sustain and reproduce this massively homogeneous pro-market City culture?

The present argument is based on a rejection of any theory of socialisation which explains ideological orientation by reference solely to the broad determining influence of collective attributes like social class origins and gender. C. Wright Mills[1] criticised the sociology of knowledge for failing to develop a detailed sense of how minds are formed by social processes. He was calling for a new social psychology. The present chapter is not concerned to develop a psychological basis for the theory of socialisation but the argument, like that of Mills, is that a detailed sense of how individuals are formed both by the broad influences of social structures and by their individual experiences is a priority for sociologists. In particular, we know little about how the pro-market orientation is formed. Among sociologists, only Max Weber has much to say about this matter in his work[2] on the origins of the 'spirit of capitalism' and the comparative sociology of religion. It is not, of course, being suggested that sociologists have achieved nothing in the way of an understanding of the details of socialisation. Clearly, for example, feminist sociologists have in the last decade or so produced significant research about the formation of gender identity. Such work examines in detail the social processes which constitute the identity of girls and boys.[3] In chapter 4, it was shown that 'modest' social class origins are not associated overall with greater doubts about market than are more 'privileged' social class origins. What we require is an understanding, similar to that achieved for gender identity, of how individuals – including, as was shown in chapter 4, many from social classes who are normally thought to favour state intervention to control or replace markets – develop strong pro-market views. The ideas developed below are no more than a tentative beginning to an essential task for contemporary sociologists.

2 THE DYNAMICS OF SOCIALISATION INTO CITY CULTURE

It seems that the City both attracts and selects individuals who are enthusiastic about markets. The subsequent experiences of these individuals, first as participants in financial markets and secondly as individuals confronted by the unity and intolerance of City culture, removes or silences any doubts they may have about the general efficacy of markets.

First, individuals who are similarly situated within an economic institution are subject to the same constraints whatever the differences in their social class origins, ideology or gender. Such differences tend to be levelled by the immediacy and power of the forces of supply and demand in volatile financial markets. The volatility of markets, in which prices are constantly changing and in which participants are brutally exposed to the immediacy of market forces, compels individuals to conform to the logic of the market if they wish to survive. They are, and experience themselves as, virtually powerless creatures of the market: success depends on 'getting the market right' or acting faster than competitors. They are impressed by the domination exerted by market forces and by the apparent efficiency of financial markets in responding to the forces of supply and demand for capital and foreign currency. In such circumstances, is it any surprise that few participants in the financial markets are able to articulate major doubts about the workings of markets? Furthermore, the logic of the market is underpinned by the enormous incentive of high earnings. Conformity is necessary for survival and brings great financial rewards.

Secondly, City firms do not rely solely on the immediacy of the market to socialise and constrain recruits. Consensus – the agreement on ideological fundamentals – is never a purely spontaneous outcome of socio-economic processes. To a large degree consensus is the consequence of the conscious intervention of powerful élites, classes or organisations. Those who possess power are able to affect what others think and do. They can achieve such results both by what they say and how they act and through the impersonal structures of institutions and organisations. Impersonal structures include matters like the formal procedures of recruitment programmes and the formally organised syllabus taught to trainees. The powerful can in a wide range of ways constrain what others think and do. The implication of this line of thought is that socialisation is a finely grained process or, to put it differently, it is constituted out of an enormous number of day-to-day interactions. Furthermore, socialisation – including adult socialisation into occupational worlds like the City – is a dynamic process, that is, a process in time. Overall, then, the socialisation to which City recruits are subjected is one which cannot be understood if one works only with a few rather crude collective attributes such as social class origin and gender. Instead, it is essential to investigate the detailed character of the processes involved. Finally, it is necessary to see that socialisation involves conflict, especially in so far as non-conformist recruits are concerned.

Recruits take time to become the kind of individuals who fit effectively into organisations. How does the process take place? Socialisation has both formal and informal aspects. The former include applications for posts, selection interviews, explicit training programmes. The latter includes the everyday interactions and contexts in which City recruits learn informally about what is, in practice, acceptable or suspect or prohibited behaviour. In this discussion, we focus not on the formal programmes of selection and training but on the informal processes. These informal processes are virtually invisible to insiders because they take them for granted as unquestionable features of City life. Such informal processes are bound up to a large degree with the affirmation of the virtues of the market principle and its defence against those misguided or malevolent outsiders who wish to regulate or replace market processes. The message to recruits – and few seem to doubt it – is 'Markets always work!'.

Let us begin at the point where recruits are selected. The City projects an image which must repel and attract potential recruits selectively. One of the many things we do not know about the City – because of the paucity of sociological research on this area – is how many people, who are otherwise interested in financial markets, lose interest because of the complacent and robust pro-market image which the City exudes. Certainly, in terms of the results, recruits appear to be a rigorously selected group in ideological terms. Such restrictiveness in terms of ideology must be a product both of selection by firms and self-selection of potential recruits.

3   CONFORMITY AND DISSENT

What about those individuals who find the ideological conformity of City culture difficult or impossible to accept? The problem for anyone who wishes to investigate those individuals who decide not to enter City posts or are not accepted because they do not fit in ideologically is that they are not working in the City but are, instead, scattered in a range of unknown occupations. It must be left to later research to determine the characteristics of such individuals. In the case of the minority of recruits who enter the City with less than strong pro-market views, we have some evidence. Some stay on, as should be clear from chapters 2, 4 and 5. Others – how many it is impossible to say – presumably leave because they find the stifling pro-market conformity intolerable. In the present context, one can only speculate about the factors which encourage recruits to leave. The writer did speak to one former stockbroker who had left because she found the unchallenged prevalence of pro-market views distressing, especially as this was allied with deeply sexist practices among her male colleagues. She left despite the fact that, in her early to mid-20s she was earning twice as much as a university professor without even having taken a university degree. It must be emphasised that in the course of research the writer had discussions with well over a hundred individuals in the City, that is, considerably more than those formally interviewed. Only one out of many recent recruits spoken to expressed any open discontent with his work and even he was not leaving the City but was moving from market-making to stockbroking. He found jobbers crude and preferred the more intellectual atmosphere of investment analysis in a stockbroking firm.

Nevertheless, the trainee period and after must be a time of conflict for all dissidents, whether they leave or stay and whether they speak out or are silent. Those who decide to remain must normally keep a low profile if they wish to have a reasonable prospect of advancement. Speaking out leads to arguments and inhibits career advancement; silence leads to a loss of self-esteem.

The narrow range of ideology among the youngest individuals (20–29 age group) was demonstrated in chapter 4 where we saw that young interviewees are very pro-market. To what extent this agreement on ideological fundamentals is present from the start or is, rather, the consequence of City socialisation processes is a matter which cannot be resolved in the present study. However, given the strong pro-market views even of the newest recruits interviewed, there seems little doubt that City socialisation processes work on extraordinarily fertile ground: that is, recruits are strongly inclined to receive pro-market ideologies uncritically.

The processes through which recruits learn about the limits of the acceptable must be partly unconscious and partly deliberate on the part of all involved, recruits and others. It is likely that the ideological – as opposed to the behavioural – aspects of socialisation are effectively unconscious. In large measure particular aspects of behaviour – for example, in relation to corporate clients – will be explicitly taught or learnt by example. Ideology is more likely to be tacitly rather than explicitly learned. This does not mean that the doubters and the dissenters, however slight their disagreement, are not made aware in one way or the other just how narrow the limits are in respect of acceptable ideologies. This should be clear from the discussion in chapter 4 of the way in which City culture stifles dissenting voices and consequently allows the pro-market consensus to remain unchallenged. Clearly the ideologically closed world of the City is very effective at consolidating pro-market views and silencing dissenting voices.

But conformity is not merely a matter of ideology, values, beliefs. It is also encouraged by other features of City life, in particular, its exclusiveness. A partner in a stockbroking firm stated[4] that City people live in 'a very enclosed world' and 'don't mix much with outsiders'. This leads, he believes to outsiders holding 'stereotypes' about the City which City people 'don't bother to attack'. There is another way of approaching this matter: City people are so cut off from the rest of British society, by their standard of living and as a result of their exclusiveness, that they have little interest in what outsiders think except when they are directly threatened. Although the stockbroker is right about the widespread ignorance of how financial markets work, he is wrong in believing that the only problem involved is for the City to learn to take the trouble to undermine stereotypes of the City by 'providing information about what they do' (in the words of the stockbroker). There is a far greater problem of which this stockbroker and almost all his City colleagues are unaware: the City itself needs to learn from those outside the City about how often market processes are inadequate from the point of view of those who are not protected by high City incomes.

The City exclusiveness just mentioned breeds and protects conformism. Nowhere is this more obvious than in sphere of dress in which the insistence on a narrow range of acceptable fashion is significant. It may seem that conformity in dress – enforced or otherwise – is a relatively trivial matter but it is not. Such conformity is one visible sign of the strict limits on what people can do, think and how they should look. It should be noted, however, that the increasing number of women in career positions makes the position more ambiguous. Some appear less constrained by such conformity. Others, especially those who work in banks or top stockbroking outfits often seem to imitate male styles. The position of men is, however, not in doubt. Wherever they are in the City (banks, market-making firms, and so on) they are normally expected to wear smart, good quality, dark business suits and black shoes with laces. It is only in exceptional cases, for example in certain market-making firms, that it is possible for dealers (although not top management) to get away with light-coloured suits, slip-on shoes and other departures from the norm. Two areas in which men are permitted to exhibit a range of colours are shirts, where a certain ostentation (including loud stripes) is often admired, and rather flamboyant braces. However, this latitude in respect of shirts and braces does not apply (among the firms studied) to banks, nor to the stuffier firms in other sectors.

The following account shows how fiercely stepping out of line in the area of dress can be treated. An interviewee described how a very young man in his first job in a leading merchant bank, working in the department dealing with large corporate clients, had worn his only, somewhat shabby suit continuously for three weeks. One day the director in charge called right across the floor, which meant that everyone in the department heard, 'Get yourself a new suit!'. This anecdote illustrates the intolerant nature of City life.[5]

4   SUMMARY

To summarise, the argument is that the manner in which recruits are socialised into City values, beliefs and ways of behaving helps us to understand why there is such a high a degree of conformity, in particular ideological conformity, in the City. Effectively, the process is finely grained: it consists of subtle hints, pressures of various degrees of severity, and occasional savagery. Finally, the experience of working in financial markets is a significant factor moulding ideological conceptions and assumptions. Moreover, the framework is buttressed by the high incomes which are a considerable incentive to believe in markets or – at the very least, in the case of the dissident minority – to conform outwardly. The cumulative impact of all these factors produces an occupational world free of fundamental dissent and, consequently, characterised by a deep complacency as to the nature of economic reality. It is in this closed, deeply intolerant world that strong pro-market views flourish.

NOTES

1.   C. Wright Mills, *Power, Politics and People* (ed.: I. L. Horowitz): 'Language, Logic and Culture' (see pp. 425–6).
2.   See: M. Weber, *The Protestant Ethic and the Spirit of Capitalism*; M. Weber, *Economy and Society*, i: chapter VI, xv; R. Bendix, *Max Weber: An intellectual portrait*: chapter V, section E.

3. See, for instance: A. Oakley, *Subject Women*: chapters 5 and 6; S. Sharpe, *'Just Like a Girl': how girls learn to be women*.
4: Taped interview: 139.
5. Taped interview: 201. This interviewee talked about the necessity of 'dressing for success' if one wishes to progress in the highly competitive world of the top merchant banks.

7 Summary, Conclusions and Implications

1 INTRODUCTION

In this chapter, section 2 summarises the analyses and findings of the study. Sections 3 and 4 examine the bearing of this research on our understanding of the contemporary British 'new right', of which the phenomenon of 'Thatcherism' is the predominant element. Section 3 is a critique of one of the most influential analytical approaches to 'Thatcherism', namely the work of Stuart Hall. Section 4 presents a different, albeit (and like Hall's perspective partial) view of the strategy of the Conservative government. Finally, section 5 discusses three significant implications of this study for future sociological research.

2 SUMMARY

This study has examined financial markets, and the ideologies which mould the perceptions of participants in these markets. Pro-market ideology, especially Neo-liberalism, has been the focus of attention: this ideology is based upon a belief in the general superiority of the market over alternative methods of organising economies.

Throughout, data have been drawn from a fieldwork study of participants in financial markets, especially The Stock Exchange. The various chapters have described and analysed key features of financial markets and of the elements which comprise the pro-market ideology.

Chapter 1 introduced the themes of the study. It outlined the main features of financial markets in order to contrast financial and product markets. Financial markets are volatile with continuous – sometimes big, sometimes rapid – price changes: they place participants in an immediate, brutal relationship with market forces; they promote a short-term logic in the minds of participants. Product markets involve greater fixed investment over longer time spans and prices tend to change less frequently:

they promote longer-term strategies. Participants in financial markets ignore this distinction between financial and product markets: they assume that all markets work in the same way as financial markets. They generalise about how economies should be organised on the basis of their knowledge and first hand experience of one kind of market. Chapter 1 introduced arguments about (a) how these pro-market views are sustained and (b) the ideological implications of these pro-market views. Finally, the chapter outlined certain features of the wider British political context since 1945. The pro-market views of the City must be located within this context – a context which has always included a vigorous debate about the desirable relationship between market and state – if they are to be adequately analysed.

Chapter 2 examined the opinions of interviewees about privatisation, progressive income taxation and unemployment. Although the questions asked were not directly about whether or not they believe in the general superiority of the market, they do (as explained in the introduction to chapter 2) allow us to infer a great deal about what the interviewees do believe about markets. Almost all interviewees assume that private ownership, competition and efficiency go hand in hand: private ownership is inseparable from competition and competition leads to efficiency. For interviewees, the obverse is that public ownership destroys or undermines competition, with resulting inefficiency. The vast majority of interviewees refuse to accept that competition and efficiency are possible when firms are publicly owned and/or where the market is regulated or replaced in certain respects. Interviewees, with few exceptions, assume that all markets (including product markets, health care, and so on) are or could be as efficient as they believe financial markets to be. They generalise from their experience of financial markets to all economic sectors in a manner which, as argued in chapter 1, is illegitimate.

Chapter 3 extended the analysis of pro-market views by investigating participants' subjective experience of financial markets. Financial markets are flex-price markets where prices change continuously and where participants stand in an immediate relationship to market forces. The consciousness of participants and their hour-by-hour activity is determined by these features of financial markets. In particular, the volatility of financial markets means that 'keeping in touch with the market' is central to the work of particpants (professional investors, stockbrokers, market-makers, and so on). The positive view of the market mechanism in general displayed by participants flows from their experience of the 'efficiency' of financial markets, that is, the speed with which prices respond to the changing balance of supply and demand in financial markets. What is more, the characteristics of individual participants are well attuned to the environment of rapidly changing, often brutal, market forces. The structure of markets compels individuals to compete and, for this reason, financial institutions select individuals who believe in the market and have immense ambition to earn high incomes and, as a result, are more likely to thrive in the insecure environment of financial markets.

Chapter 3 also analysed the subjective meaning of the market for participants in financial markets through an examination of data about what they liked about their work. Participants enjoy working in markets: indeed, they are excited by the risks involved and by the high level of activity of those around them. For example, individuals who worked on the floor of The Stock Exchange spoke, both in interviews and in casual conversation, about how stimulating they found it when business was brisk or hectic. Similarly, individuals in the dealing rooms talked about the excitement of a fast moving market. In general interviewees admired the energy and ambition of those involved in financial markets.

Chapter 4 was a tentative attempt to account for the predominance in the City of the pro-market orientation. The question posed is how we can account for the extraordinary commitment of interviewees to the institution of the market. Evidence presented suggests that recruits enter the City with strong pro-market views. Their belief in the market cannot be reduced to the influence of their social class of origin. Data examined show that individuals from 'modest' social class backgrounds (state school education, fathers in occupations outside social classes 1 and 2) are about as pro-market as those from more 'privileged' backgrounds. This suggests that social class cannot be the only factor constituting an individual's ideology. Other factors, relating both to collective attributes of groups and to individual experience, determine ideologies.[1]

It must be emphasised that the argument is not that social class is an unimportant factor in determining ideology. The wealthy have disproportionate power and enormous influence over the media, education, and so on. Similarly, the culture of the City of London into which recruits are socialised is the result of centuries of domination by the wealthy and the landed who, of course, favour the market. However, an adequate sociological conceptualisation of the development of the ideologies of individuals and groups must go beyond linking ideology to social class.

Socialisation both in the wider society and into City culture is a finely grained process which must be influenced by numerous factors.[2] The analysis in chapter 4 draws attention to some of the factors which affect individuals, both throughout their lives and during their time in the City. Chapter 3 had already indicated that part of the explanation for the predominance of pro-market views lies in the nature of financial markets and in the characteristics of those who are attracted to work in such markets. In addition, working in markets is, as explained in chapter 3, exciting and often intrinsically rewarding and this encourages a positive view of markets.

In chapter 4, particular attention was paid to the constraining features of work in financial markets: their volatility and competitiveness make it difficult for those who are not committed to the market to survive. It is likely that this powerful pressure to believe in the market helps to strengthen and sustain the pro-market commitments of participants. Furthermore, normally, only those who conform ideologically, that is, hold strong pro-market views, are recruited and build successful careers. City culture is intolerant of deviance on this score. Criticism of the market is virtually tabooed. Non-conformists are filtered out (often, the writer suspects, they leave of their own accord) or remain silent because to speak up is inimical to one's career and leads to unpleasant arguments. Finally, all participants, even the few who do have doubts about the general superiority of the market, desire the enormous material rewards that go to those who are successful – and success, needless to say, is partly dependent on ideological conformity.

Chapter 5 examines the implications of pro-market views. The chapter analyses a range of ideologies and how proponents of each ideology conceive the socio-economic arrangements of society. Data are presented which demonstrate that over half of the interviewees adhere to views close to or coincident with

Neo-liberal ideology. Neo-liberal ideology is the systematic working out of the pro-market orientation. In fact, 86 per cent of interviewees – those classified Neo-liberal, 'between Neo-liberalism and Traditional Conservatism' and Traditional Conservative – wish to dismantle all or many of the key elements of the post-1945 British consensus: all are very pro-market by British standards. Overall, the conclusion of this study as a whole that robust pro-market views dominate City culture is in line with the widespread view of the City as a place dominated by the 'more pure and limited capitalist viewpoint' (in the words of the quotation that heads chapter 5). The empirical validity of this view of the City has been demonstrated on the basis of interviews with a widely varied selection of participants.

Chapter 6 was a brief and speculative discussion of the City socialisation process. First of all, an appeal is made for a theory of socialisation which eschews explanation simply in terms of the determining influence of social class or other collective attributes. Instead, our picture of socialisation should do justice to its finely grained and complex nature. The ideological conformity of City life is in part the product of the nature of financial markets. The study as a whole has emphasised the forceful effects of involvement in financial markets on the behaviour and thought of participants: participants experience the tremendous impersonal power of the market and are impressed by what they see as its efficiency. In addition, the high earnings associated with work in financial markets are an incentive to believe in the market. The chapter then turns to the specific issue of the (adult) socialisation of recruits to City firms. How does the City socialise recruits? Several significant features of City culture are isolated for analysis. First, the City projects an image of itself which selectively attracts and repels potential recruits. This effect is compounded by the fact that City firms appear to recruit, with few exceptions, only those who are strongly pro-market. The trainee confronts a culture which is homogeneously and complacently pro-market. Those few recruits who dissent ideologically leave or keep silent. Silence is, with few exceptions, the only option for the non-conformist who wishes to remain. City culture leaves little in the way of a foothold for the emergence of critical ideas. The argument of chapter 6 is not that City firms explicitly indoctrinate recruits. It is likely that the processes are largely tacit. Individuals learn, almost unconciously, that certain thoughts are acceptable and others are not.

3 HALL'S ANALYSIS OF 'THATCHERISM': A CRITIQUE

This research has a bearing on an understanding of the phenomenon of the contemporary British 'new' or 'radical' right which is frequently called 'Thatcherism'. Mrs Thatcher's domination of the Conservative Party has been associated with a distinctive blend[3] of Neo-liberal views about state intervention in markets and more conventional conservative themes of 'tradition, family and nation, respectability, patriarchalism and order'. Much analysis of the British radical right has been in terms of its alleged success in winning the battle of ideas. Perhaps, the most influential interpretation (and not just among Marxists) is that of Stuart Hall. In his view, 'Thatcherism' is a response to a deep and long-running 'organic crisis' of British society. The Thatcherite strategy is a total one[4]:

> . . . Thatcherite politics are 'hegemonic' in their conception and project: the aim is to struggle on several fronts at once, not on the economic-corporate one alone; and this is based on the knowledge that, in order really to dominate and restructure a social formation, political, moral and intellectual leadership must be coupled to economic dominance.

In Hall's view, the radical right understands, unlike the left, that ideas have to be taken seriously. In particular, the radical right rejects the view that[5]:

> ideas are determined by material and economic conditions. They actually do believe that you have to struggle to implant the notion of the market; and that, if you talk about it well enough, effectively and persuasively enough, you can touch people's understanding of how they live and work, and make a new kind of sense about what's wrong with society and what to do about it.

Hall wishes to avoid (amongst other errors) 'economism': the belief that ideas are determined by economic structures and interests.[6] Accordingly, he focuses on the crucial importance of ideology and politics: the left, like the radical right, has to construct a hegemonic politics or, as he expressed it in an article[7] written after the 1987 General Election, offer voters a broad 'image' of a society with which they can identify. Hall states in this post-election commentary that although ideology does not determine everything – 'Thatcherism' appeals because it has offered many individuals greater prosperity – material interests are always 'ideologically defined'.

The problem with Hall's analysis is not that he takes ideas and politics too seriously but that he does not take the power of the economic element seriously enough. The present study has again and again reiterated the argument that financial markets powerfully constrain participants and significantly influence the ideas they hold. To a degree Hall recognises this[8]:

> Gramsci always insisted that hegemony is not exclusively an ideological phenomenon. There can be no hegemony without 'the decisive nucleus of the economic'. On the other hand, do not fall into the trap of the old mechanical economism and believe that if you can only get hold of the economy, you can move the rest of life.

Hall also notes[9] that the force of pro-market ideas is based on the fact that:

> After all, under capitalism, men and women *do* live their lives and sell their labour, every day, in the market.

However, the overall thrust of his analysis, despite his occasional references to the importance of the economic element, is an exaggeration of the success of 'Thatcherism' in winning the ideological battle. He has on occasion recognised that many Thatcherite ideas are out of tune with British public opinion. For example, in 1986 he wrote[10] that the Conservative government's partial change of policy on public spending in that year was the result of the fact that it had been obliged to accept that the vast majority of voters favoured increases in public spending on health, education and social security benefits. However, his usual approach is substantially different. For example, in 1987 he stated[11] that there are no prospects for the revival of old-style interventionist reformism because 'Nobody believes in it any more. Its material conditions have disappeared'. In fact, as the review of public opinion in chapter 2 of this study (and the public opinion surveys on which it is based) make clear, there is a wide gap between the Conservative government's policies and majority public opinion on a number of key issues. As Parekh notes[12]:

> Almost all the public attitude surveys show that the bulk of the country remains committed to non-Thatcherite values.

Overall, despite Hall's occasional recognition of the significance of the economic element, his analysis understates the constraints and influences of economic forces on what people do and think. Although, initially his new emphasis on the critical importance of politics and ideology was a welcome development within the British left – because it forces the left to confront the reasons for the contemporary sterility of their traditional strategy – it is essential that the fundamentally formative character of the economic element is recognised. Ultimately, an adequate overall analysis will require the integration of economics, politics, ideology and culture. For present purposes, it is enough to reinstate the economic element.

4   MARKETS, IDEOLOGY AND THE 'NEW RIGHT'

Here is another (tentative) view of the Thatcherite strategy. Like Hall's it is a partial view[13] but, all the same, a necessary corrective to his emphasis on ideology. It begins with a recognition that 'Thatcherism' has been far less successful ideologically than Hall contends. The argument formulated here is about the implicit strategy of Mrs Thatcher's government in the light of the contention of the present study that unmediated exposure to market forces in volatile financial markets seems to be associated with a belief in the general efficacy of markets. What is the implication of this association between exposure to market forces and belief in the market for an understanding of what Mrs Thatcher and her associates are trying to achieve? Is the government gambling on the general effectiveness of the relationship between exposure to market forces and pro-market views?

Government policies represent a deliberate attempt to remove most market regulation of whatever kind (for example, subsidies, public ownership of industry, incomes policy, trade union power) in order to subject as many individuals as possible to the full impact of market forces. Presumably, the assumption is that in this way individuals will be persuaded that the virtues and efficiencies of the market, so often proclaimed by the proponents of Neo-liberalism, are indeed a reality. Do they seek to dismantle much of the machinery of state intervention and regulation not just because they dislike such machinery *per se*, but because, like laboratory scientists working on a giant scale, they are trying to produce a particular effect by manipulating crucial variables? If this is the government's approach, their assumption would be that individuals who were previously prisoners of 'collectivist' ideologies will learn to appreciate the virtues of markets if they are exposed to unregulated and (so the theory goes) consequently successful markets. Does this explain the government's enthusiasm for the growth of the financial sector? In other words, is the growing involvement, encouraged by the state, of the small private investor (insurance policies, shareholdings, and so forth) in the financial markets calculated to contribute decisively to the desired shift in behaviour, values and ideas?

If the answer to all the questions in the preceding paragraph is 'Yes', then we are faced with an irony. The new right, the great enemy of Marxism (which is always claimed by the right to be economic determinist), is relying – to a considerable degree – on economic factors (the influence of market forces) to produce a change in values and beliefs amongst the British population. The Thatcher strategy is then, in larger measure than Hall's analysis allows, to change the economic institutions so that a desirable shift of ideology will follow. In terms of this interpretation, Sir Geoffrey Howe's statement of principles as new Chancellor of the Exchequer in 1979 is fascinating.[14]

First, 'We need to strengthen incentives . . .': this entails a clear relationship between contribution to the market and earnings. Second, 'We need to enlarge freedom of choice for the individual by reducing the role of the state . . . ': that is, individuals should make their own choices in the market and should not rely on state provision. The third and fourth principles refer respectively to the need to reduce the financial 'burden' of state expenditure to 'leave room for commerce and industry to prosper' and the need to make workers aware of the consequences of pay demands and settlements. In both cases, the goal is to open the economy up to market forces.

In summary, whatever the particular policy initiatives (tax changes, weakening of trade unions, privatisation, reduction of civil service staffing, and so on), a major overall aim of the Thatcher government is to change economic behaviour and encourage the values and beliefs which underpin the 'enterprise culture'. Policies which force individuals to confront market forces are a crucial means to the desired change in values.[15]

It is, however, doubtful that the strategy of exposing

individuals to markets in order to change values will be as successful as the government may hope. The reason – and this was discussed in chapter 1 – is that financial markets are very different from product markets. First, prices in financial markets move rapidly and continuously in response to changes in supply and demand and this is possible partly because such markets do not involve the massive long-term investments typical of many product markets. Product markets cannot therefore be left to the mercy of free, competitive markets without devastating both the lives of citizens and the industries of a country as happened in the first half of the 1980s. Second, competition takes very different forms in financial markets and product markets. In the former, competition takes the form of arbitrage, that is, is mainly about relative returns in different financial markets or from different financial instruments. In product markets, competition takes the form of creative destruction: firms invest because they can only compete effectively if they have the latest technology; the alternative to investment is extinction.

These fundamental differences between financial markets and product markets may explain why so many British citizens reject key government policies. Financial markets can more easily be seen as efficient at achieving the goals of investors – although by no means always – while product markets are seen by many to cry out for various forms of state intervention which the government rejects.

5 IMPLICATIONS FOR FUTURE SOCIOLOGICAL RESEARCH

This research has three major implications. First, that sociologists should investigate, both theoretically and empirically, the origins and dynamics of pro-market views, a subject about which little is known. The findings of this study make some contribution to the understanding of how such views are nourished and strengthened in the City financial markets and in the community within which these markets operate. However, further research is essential if the factors producing pro-market views in a variety of contexts, that is, not just in financial markets, are to be understood.

Second, further sociological research on how financial markets work is required. Since financial markets play a crucial – and increasingly important – role in advanced capitalist societies, sociologists should make a genuine attempt to discover what they can contribute to an understanding of these markets. It is depressing that recent sociology has almost nothing to say about the origins and dynamics of pro-market views and the functioning of financial markets. Both are fundamental aspects of capitalist society. The absence of sociological interest in these two subjects should be treated as a problem in the sociology of (sociological) knowledge.

Third, the study highlights the need for substantive research on ideologies. Recently, social scientists have begun to carry out impressive work on social attitudes – what people believe about equality, privatisation, sexuality and morality and other critical issues. (Some of this work was reviewed at the end of chapter 2.) Despite this welcome development, substantive research on the factors involved in the origins and formation of the ideologies (especially their socio-political aspects) of individuals, classes, genders, ethnic minorities and others is lacking.

NOTES

1. Unfortunately, sociologists have little to contribute to our understanding of the formation of ideologies. Empirical research projects – perhaps, along the lines advocated in chapter 6 – are essential if we are to develop a greater knowledge of the relevant factors.

2. These ideas have been developed in long conversations with Andrew Graham of Balliol College, Oxford.

3. S. Hall, *The Hard Road to Renewal*: p. 2. This book collects together a number of his essays. See also A. Gamble, *The Free Economy and the Strong State: The Politics of Thatcherism*: chapter 2 (especially, p. 60).

4. Hall, *The Hard Road to Renewal*: p. 154 (in the essay 'Authoritarian Populism: A Reply to Jessop *et al.*').

5. Hall, *The Hard Road to Renewal*: p. 188 (in 'The Battle for Socialist Ideas in the 1980s').

6. Hall, *The Hard Road to Renewal*: p. 3 ('Introduction' to the collection of essays).

7. Hall, *The Hard Road to Renewal*: pp. 260–2 ('Blue Election, Election Blues').

8. Hall, *The Hard Road to Renewal*: p. 170 (in 'Gramsci and.Us').

9. Hall, *The Hard Road to Renewal*: p. 189 (in 'The Battle for Socialist Ideas in the 1980s').

10. Hall, *The Hard Road to Renewal*: p. 81 (in 'No Light at the End of the Tunnel').

11. Hall, *The Hard Road to Renewal*: p. 172 (in 'Gramsci and Us').

12.   B. Parekh, 'How not to be a Thatcherite', *New Statesman & Society*, 16 December 1988. This review of Hall's book greatly influenced the final version of this part of chapter 7.

13.   In the introduction to *The Hard Road to Renewal*, Hall appears to accept that his essays on 'Thatcherism' do represent a less than 'comprehensive analysis of Thatcherism'. He states that the essays 'provide no substantive assessment of Thatcherism's economic policy, though in fairness they cannot be said to neglect the economic dimension' (p. 3). He justifies his focus on ideology and politics as a deliberate strategy to emphasise the need for the left to avoid 'economism' and other errors.

14.   P. Donaldson, *A Question of Economics*: p. 38.

15.   This interpretation of the Thatcher government's strategy, as remarked earlier, is partial not only in that it discusses the economic element in isolation from the explicitly political and ideological battle: it ignores also, and this is because this study focuses on markets, the conventional conservative emphases on social order, 'traditional' morality, and so on which are integral to 'Thatcherism'. The aim of the argument which has been developed in this chapter has already been explained but the point needs reiteration in order to avoid misunderstanding: it is necessary that the economic element be reinstated in social analysis; the pendulum has swung too far in favour of ideology, culture and politics. Sociological analysis must incorporate the economic element as well as the elements just mentioned.

Appendix 1: Fieldwork Methods

Three formal methods were used to collect data: semi-structured interviews; a questionnaire for completion by interviewees; and direct observation. These methods were supplemented by informal observation.

1 INTERVIEWS

Interviews were organised around a series of previously selected topics. The initial questions asked on each topic were pre-formulated but, in practice, were varied according to circumstances and the individual. Similarly, a number of follow-up questions for each topic were pre-formulated but these too were adapted to individuals. The emphasis was on the desirability of responding flexibly to individuals; this affected both the wording of questions in interviews, the willingness of the researcher to allow interviewees to speak on unanticipated topics and the time spent on each topic.

Interviews were used to gather information about a wide range of matters: (a) the social class background of individuals as indicated by both parents' occupations; (b) how the individual was recruited to the City and why she or he decided on a City career; (c) the character of the individual's work; (d) what the individual liked and disliked about her or his work; (e) what newspapers, weeklies and magazines the interviewee read on a regular basis; and finally, (f) the socio-political opinions of the interviewee.

Much of the information about recruitment and why the individual chose a City career was not used in this study but will be used elsewhere if possible.

Originally, it was intended to ask questions about leisure activities and the interviewee's opinions about how best to protect investors. The former topic was dropped because it became obvious early on that it was outside the range of relevant issues for this project. The topic of investor protection was dropped, despite its importance, partly to keep the interviews short (interviewees were seldom willing to give more than 45 minutes of their time and often gave less) and partly because only those in very high positions tended to know anything about the matter – others merely had prejudices against state regulation of the financial markets. It was decided to focus instead on socio-political issues about which virtually everyone had both decided opinions and some knowledge (privatisation, income tax and, later, government policy on unemployment).

The coverage of interviews was affected by the time available and by whether the individual had been observed at work. When the interviewee had been observed at work for a sustained period (a day) and had little time for the interview, the questions about what she or he did at work were dropped. This exclusion affected only market-makers, principally those working on the floor of The Stock Exchange. Every interviewee was asked about how and why she or he entered the City, what she or he liked and disliked about the job and her or his opinions about the socio-political issues. Variations in the coverage of interviews not only reflected the time available but also what the interviewee had to say. It was usually fruitful to allow an interviewee to talk for a limited period about what particularly interested or concerned her or him. Frequently, these parts of the interview were very valuable and they enabled a better relationship to be built up between interviewer and interviewee. In fact, it was as a result of this flexibility that the researcher became aware of the crucial importance of the concept of markets for organising the whole project and not just parts of it – originally the idea was to split the study up into three parts (People, Work in Markets, Ideology), each part organised around different research preoccupations. Increasingly, the researcher noticed that interviewees talked again and again about the techniques they used for keeping abreast of the market and became aware that the initial concern with whether people spent time writing, in meetings, dealing with others and so on was of secondary importance.

The original idea was to interview for an hour to an hour-and-a-half. Most City people regarded this as unrealistic and requests for interviews of 30 to 40 minutes became standard. Interviews with jobbers and a few stockbrokers were shorter than this but, in the case of jobbers, they had usually been observed at work for at least a day. A disquieting problem was that individuals would change their minds about the time they had available during the interview or would announce changes to arrangements when the researcher arrived. Such alterations worked both ways: usually interviews were longer than promised but on a few occasions they were shorter.

2   THE QUESTIONNAIRE

Each interviewee was asked to complete a one-page questionnaire and all but one did so. The questionnaire is included at the end of this Appendix. The aim was to collect data about the individual's education, career to date, age, marital status and number of children. The latter two items were not used. The information on education was very helpful for allocating an individual to social class of origin on the basis of type of school attended. The age breakdown was essential for parts of chapters 4, 5 and 6.

3   DIRECT OBSERVATION

Although most data was collected through interviews and questionnaires the periods of direct observation were very valuable. In the early stages, the researcher had ambitious plans to spend a week or a month in each of several offices. Early lack of success with requests to sit in and observe (later requests were successful) led to a reappraisal of the role of observation in the project. It became clear that observational material was useful for understanding how participants worked in the markets but that it was unlikely to be effective for learning about socio-political opinions. For this reason, great care was taken to keep periods of observation down to manageable proportions. Seven full days were spent on the floor of The Stock Exchange and (before and after Stock Exchange business hours) in the dealing rooms of four Stock Exchange firms. A day was spent in the dealing room of a small merchant bank.

4   INFORMAL OBSERVATION

Informal observation in wine bars, restaurants, and the like provided further valuable information about City life including dress, drinking habits, informal behaviour and so on. Interviews themselves gave numerous opportunities for observation. Observation of the reception area and those who passed through, the room in which the interview took place (furniture, paintings), the interviewee (dress, accent, demeanour, and so on) and various other details were very revealing. Norman Denzin's[1] remark that 'a good interviewer is by necessity also a participant observer' emphasises how crucial such observation during interviews can be. Furthermore, interviewees often invited the researcher into dealing rooms and working offices (rather than meeting or interview rooms) for the interview itself, as part of a tour of the firm, to see colleagues at work, or to meet others or for coffee and a chat.[2]

NOTES

1. N. Denzin, *The Research Act: a theoretical introduction to sociological methods* (2nd edn): p. 129.
2. G. V. Stimson's 'Place and space in sociological fieldwork', *The Sociological Review*, 34: No. 3, August 1986, which was read in draft versions during the period of fieldwork, taught the author a great deal about the importance of looking – sociologists tend to listen rather than look.

THE QUESTIONNAIRE

Number ....
Age...........   Marital status ....
Number of children (if any) ....
Schools attended ....
....
Higher education institutions attended (if any) ....
....
Qualifications, (e.g., number of O Levels, CSEs, A Levels; Professional
Qualifications; Diplomas; Degrees, etc.) ....
....
Current Position...

	Post	
	Name of firm	
	Number of years in post	
Previous Positions	(1)	Post held..
		Type of organisation (e.g., stockbroker)
		....
		Number of years ....
	(2)	Post held..
		Type of organisation...........................
		Number of years ....
	(3)	Post held..
		Type of organisation...........................
		Number of years ....

If you have held more than three positions, please give details on the back of this sheet.

Thank you for taking the trouble to complete this questionnaire.

Appendix 2:   Selection of Interviewees

1   INTRODUCTION

One hundred and three interviews were carried out, two individuals being interviewed twice and one person being interviewed merely about technical aspects of 'hedging' Gilt-edged securities (that is, offsetting the financial risk associated with holding these securities) by buying futures on LIFFE (London International Financial Futures Exchange). After completing the fieldwork, two individuals were removed from the group of interviewees to be included in the analysis leaving 98 interviewees. The two interviewees removed were occupants of lowly clerical and technical posts unlike all the others in the sample who were on a 'career' ladder with prospects of extremely high earnings and some possibility of becoming directors, partners or senior managers.

It would not have been effective for an unknown researcher to decide upon the boundaries of the sampling universe, select a statistically representative sample and fire off written requests for interviews. City people would not, with the (possible) exception of unrepresentative intellectuals, respond well to a request letter from an unknown individual. Virtually every interviewee was approached on the basis of some kind of personal connection, however tenuous. At first, it was difficult to find interviewees but as the work progressed, more interviewees became available. Increasingly, the problem was to find the right kind of interviewees rather than merely to interview everyone who was available.

It is not possible to produce a statistically representative sample unless one possesses accurate data about the population to be sampled, including its boundaries. A rigorously representative sample would need to take account of all kinds of differences between financial institutions (size, type of ownership, organisational structure, prestige of firm, specialist activities, and so on) as well as significant distinctions between individuals (education, social class origins, age, gender, ethnic origin, and the

147

like). Sociological knowledge of the City is so poor that we just do not possess the relevant information. Furthermore, the concept of 'the City' is so ambiguous that we could never produce a strictly representative, 'probability', sample of City people. Additionally, crucial terms are imprecise: for example, the definition of 'merchant banks' used by some writers (for example, Clay and Whebble[1]) includes only the members of the élite Accepting Houses Committee; many merchant banks such as Barclays Merchant Bank, County Bank (owned by NatWest Bank) as well as many smaller merchant banks (for example, Close Bros. Ltd.) would have been excluded. Others, for example, the financial press adopt a more catholic understanding of the term 'merchant bank'. Definitional problems were and are further exacerbated by the rapid pace of change in the City ('the City revolution') which was and is destroying old boundaries between types of institution and leading to immense changes in the scale and behaviour of organisations.[2]

Individuals were selected for interview on the basis of considerations which changed during the course of the fieldwork. Initially, with few City contacts, the researcher took up all offers of interviews arranged by these contacts even when the individuals concerned did not work as stockbrokers, jobbers or merchant bankers. This strategy was essential as a means to gain a reasonable foothold in the City financial markets from which the project could develop. Later, selection became possible. Individuals from particular specialist groups (for instance,

TABLE A2.1 *Breakdown of interviewees by type of firm*

Type of firm	Number of individuals
Jobbing	22
Stockbroking	40
Merchant Bank	20
Clearing Bank	3
Insurance Co.	2
Venture Capital	2
US Securities House in City	3
Other*	6
Total individuals	98

*Corporate PR specialist, foreign exchange broker, unit trust fund manager, and so on.

dealers in stockbroking firms, investment analysts) or of a certain kind (non-graduates, older people, recent recruits, women) were chosen in order to take account of possibly significant variations in the City. The goal was to include as wide a range of interviewees as possible: from different kinds of firm, specialisms, backgrounds, ages, genders, financial markets. The reason for such a goal was simply that the intention was to produce as representative a sample as was possible in the circumstances.[3] The researcher was encouraged by the fact that, at the end of the fieldwork, participants in the financial markets to whom he spoke seemed to feel that the full range of variations within the three types of firm on which the research had concentrated were adequately represented.

2 BREAKDOWN OF INTERVIEWEES

The group of interviewees incorporates the following crucial variables: differences in (a) type of firm, (b) specialisation, (c) position (seniority) and (d) age. Tables A2.1 to A2.4, present breakdowns of the interviewees in terms of each of these variables.[4]

(a) Breakdown by type of firm

Financial sector terms (fund manager, and so on) used in this and subsequent tables are explained in Appendix 3.

Table A2.1 indicates that attention was concentrated on stockbrokers (40 individuals), jobbers (22) and merchant bankers (20): 82 out of 98 individuals are so categorised. The reason for this concentration was that the researcher was most interested in the firms engaged wholly or partly in The Stock Exchange; this choice was made for reasons of economy since clearly one individual could not adequately deal with all financial markets in so short a study. Other types of firms (insurance companies, and so on) were included for two reasons. First, including individuals from other sectors of the City enabled the writer to develop a better overall picture of the City. Second, in the early stages of the fieldwork, the writer was not confident that a reasonable number of stockbrokers, jobbers and merchant bankers would be forthcoming: therefore, as an insurance all willing individuals were interviewed. Later, even when it was clear that enough of the three preferred groups were available the writer continued to interview individuals working for other types of firm in accordance with the wish to gain a sense of the financial markets of the City as a whole.

(b) Specialisation

The selected interviewees incorporate all the major specialist functions in stockbroking, jobbing and merchant banking. Indeed, every effort was made to include significant variations within specialist categories: for example, institutional salesmen dealing in both company securities (equities, preference shares,

TABLE A2.2   *Breakdown by specialisation of individuals*

Specialisation (1)	Number of individuals
Jobber Dealer	19
Stockbroker Dealer	6
Institutional Salesman	8
Private Clients	6
Investment Analysis	10
Economic Analysis	2
Fund Management	3
Corporate Finance	5
Management (2)	17
General (3)	3
Eurobonds	5
Venture Capital	3
Other (4)	11
Total individuals	98

(1) Individuals who carried out more than one function were classified according to their main function.
(2) This figure includes only those who spent most of their time on general management activities: it excludes those who were involved in management in one particular specialist area, these latter being classified under the relevant specialism (for instance, Corporate Finance). Breakdown by position (Table A2.3) provides information about the distribution of individuals throughout the hierarchy.
(3) Three individuals who carried out general stockbroking activities: all are Associate Members (self-employed) of The Stock Exchange.
(4) Category includes a foreign exchange broker and dealer, two traded options market-makers, a statistician, two personnel managers, someone engaged on theoretical work in investment analysis, and so on.

debentures, and so on) and gilt-edged (that is, government) securities were interviewed. The breakdown of the interviewees by specialisation is presented in Table A2.2

(c) **Position**

The term 'position' refers to status within the hierarchy of the firm or, in the case of the few self-employed individuals, status within the market or sector (see Table A2.3, note 1). It should be noted that terms used to describe an individual's position are not always standardised in the City: for example, some firms have enormous boards of directors and effectively junior directors are assistant directors or senior executives; other firms have small boards and very senior people will be termed senior executives. The

TABLE A2.3   *Breakdown of interviewees by position*

Position	Number of individuals
Associate Member (1)	4
Trainee (2)	9
Staff (on career ladder) (3)	28
Executive (4)	9
Senior Executive (5)	9
Partner (6)	17
Director (7)	9
Managing Director and/or Chairman (8)	13
Total individuals	98

(1) Self-employed Associate Members of The Stock Exchange; two of these employed the odd person; all worked within the confines of a stockbroking firm, using its stock clearing and office facilities in return for a share of the commission fees earned by the Associate Member.
(2) Trainees in merchant banks, stockbroking and jobbing firms.
(3) Staff who were not trainees but did not occupy positions carrying managerial responsibilities.
(4) Individuals wielding managerial functions but, unlike category (5), not situated just below main board or Partnership level.
(5) Individuals discharging managerial functions; usually just below main board level and often full Directors of wholly-owned subsidiaries of the firm.
(6) Partners: owners with unlimited liability.
(7) Main board Directors of merchant banks, incorporated firms of stockbrokers and jobbers.
(8) Individuals holding the top or one of a handful of top positions in banks, incorporated stockbroking or jobbing firms.

researcher has had to produce standardised categories and allocate individuals to them. Allocation was based on information supplied by the interviewees, house publications and the researcher's general knowledge of the City. Categorisation has, consequently, been difficult to accomplish: figures in Table A2.3 about the distribution of interviewees by position are indicative rather than precise.

(d) Age Profile

It was essential to select interviewees across the whole age range: effectively, this means those between 20 and 60. There are relatively few active participants in the financial markets who are over 60. Individuals under 20 holding career positions must be rare: graduates do not join until their early 20s or later and school leaver recruits often spend a few years in the back office before they are offered the opportunity to train as dealers, salesmen and so on. The writer met few individuals who appeared to be under 20 and they were often shyer than average. One agreed to an interview but failed to turn up and ignored subsequent telephone messages. Overall, despite the lack of representation of the under 20s, the collection of interviewees adequately reflects the age distribution. Data are presented in Table A2.4

3 SUMMARY

In summary, the interviewees selected cover all the crucial variables amongst the groups on which research was concentrated

TABLE A2.4   *Breakdown of interviewees by age*

Age Range	Number of individuals
20–29	30
30–39	27
40–49	27
50–59	11
60 and above	3
Total individuals	98

(stockbrokers, jobbers, merchant bankers). Also included are individuals who provide a wider representation of City people: individuals working in insurance companies, foreign exchange brokers and so forth. The writer is, therefore, able to echo Lupton and Wilson's remark about those they investigated in their classic article on top decision-makers:[5]

> Our choice of persons and categories was influenced by our starting point, and our enquiries were limited by considerations of time and space, and by gaps in the published sources of data. For these reasons our results are not statistically significant. But they will be of interest to sociologists . . .

It is hoped that the results of this study will be of interest not just to sociologists but to anyone with a wish or need to understand financial markets in general and the City of London in particular.

NOTES

1. C. J. J. Clay and B. S. Wheble, *Modern Merchant Banking* (2nd edn, revised by L. H. L. Cohen): pp. 9–10.
2. These changes are discussed in Appendix 3.
3. The selection procedure could be described more technically as follows. Initially, the researcher relied almost completely on 'snowball' (interviewing the contacts of interviewees) or 'opportunistic' sampling (interviewing those who offered themselves) with the intention of making the group of interviewees more representative later on. Increasingly, the opportunity to select interviewees arose and at this stage the researcher practised what Glaser and Strauss term 'theoretical' sampling (*The Discovery of Grounded Theory*: chapter 3) or what Honigmann refers to as 'judgement' sampling (J. J. Honigmann, 'Sampling in Ethnographic Fieldwork' in R. G. Burgess (ed.), *Field Research: a Sourcebook and Field Manual*). The idea was to include all categories and differences significant in the light of the research aims. Other references consulted include: R. G. Burgess, *In the Field*: chapter 3; N. Denzin, *The Research Act*: pp. 78–87; M. Hammersley and P. Atkinson, *Ethnography: Principles in Practice*: pp. 40–53.
4. Gender differences turned out not to be associated with differences in socio-political opinions. Nor did they affect how people worked or how they viewed their work. This does not mean that women have not been disadvantaged in all sorts of ways: initial recruitment, promotion prospects and sexual harassment are areas of note here. These matters are

outside the scope of the present study but the researcher hopes to pursue them elsewhere. Ethnic differences were not investigated. Black people are seldom recruited to career positions and Asians were few and far between in the firms visited (the numbers of Chinese and Japanese individuals and firms in the City are growing). The researcher did not meet any black or Asian individuals in the course of the fieldwork.

5.   T. Lupton and C. Shirley Wilson, 'The Social Background and Connections of "Top Decision Makers" ' in J. Urry and J. Wakeford (eds), *Power in Britain*.

Appendix 3: A Select Overview of City Institutions and Terminology

Britain is one of the world's great financial centres. The financial services industry contributes a growing share to the nation's wealth and to its earnings abroad. Its activities include the raising and distribution of funds to government, industry and commerce; trading in stocks and shares, in financial and commodity futures and options; the management of investment portfolios; the management and marketing of investment trusts, unit trusts, and life assurance policies.

(Government White Paper)[1]

1   INTRODUCTION

Section 2 examines the City institutions and financial markets to which reference is made in the study, even if such reference is only brief. Section 3 deals with recent and current changes in the City in so far as they affect the above institutions and markets. Sections 4 and 5 discuss the terminology of the relevant financial markets at the time of the fieldwork (1985): section 4 clarifies basic financial market terms; section 5 deals with the various specialist activities associated with dealing in stocks and shares. Section 6 outlines the Stock Exchange hierarchy in 1985 (that is, prior to 'Big Bang').

2   INSTITUTIONS AND FINANCIAL MARKETS: A SELECT OVERVIEW

(a) Merchant Banks[2]

Two-thirds of the merchant bankers interviewed worked in the most prestigious merchant banks, these being members of the

Accepting Houses Committee. This committee had 16 members in 1985, one from each member bank. Merchant banks or financial groups based upon merchant banks even before the period of the 'City Revolution', which will be discussed later, engaged in an enormous range of activities. These encompassed banking activities; issuing securities for companies; corporate finance advice; involvement in the wholesale capital markets, both domestic (Sterling money markets) and international (the euromarkets); investment management; participation in the foreign exchange markets; provision of venture capital; bullion dealing; financial advice to governments; leasing; insurance and insurance broking services; and so on.[3] It is not necessary for readers to understand every term in the list; the activities of interviewees are covered by the seven areas which are discussed below.

(i) Banking

Many of the oldest merchant banks were originally merchant enterprises which were, or became, involved in banking services. In particular merchant banks performed – and still do – a role for those who were involved in trade and needed short-term credit to finance their activities: such people could issue short-term (three-month) *Bills of Exchange* in return for the cash needed; the merchant banks providing the cash. These bills became negotiable – that is, could be bought and sold in the hope of profit – if they were 'accepted' by a reputable bank which promised to pay the amount involved if the issuer defaulted. In other words, 'acceptance' of the bill meant that buyers knew that the accepting bank had guaranteed payment. If the holder of the bill, whether the original lender or someone else, needed the cash before maturity he or she was able to sell the bill. There has always been a market in such bills in which banks and financial institutions called 'discount houses' – which will be discussed below – have been active: this market plays a key role in ensuring the liquidity of the UK banking system, as is explained below.[4] As a result of such activities, many merchant banks – not just those represented on the Accepting Houses Committee – came to be known as 'accepting houses'.

Merchant banks have a restricted capacity to lend from their own balance sheets because even the biggest have relatively small capital bases.[5] They often prefer to act as *agents* linking lenders and borrowers of funds. However, they do lend relatively small sums (by the standards of the clearing banks like Lloyds or the big foreign banks) for specific projects or transactions of corporate entities of various kinds. Merchant banks discharge specialised banking functions which may or may not involve provision of funds: help to corporations which wish to reduce their tax liability (a merchant banker described this as 'financial engineering'); advice on interest rate swaps, for example, switching from a fixed-rate to a floating-rate interest payment obligation; advice on currency swaps, for example, transferring a liability from sterling into US dollars.

(ii) Issuing

Merchant banks act also as 'issuing houses'. William Clarke explains that issuing houses:[6]

> are concerned with the issue of new securities, on behalf of commercial or governmental borrowers, on the stock market.

Merchant banks play a major role in this area. However, many issuing houses are not merchant banks; some stockbroking firms are included under this term.

(iii) Corporate finance services

Corporate finance departments advise firms on the raising of capital, how to respond to a take-over bid or a merger prospect, public relations policy and on a wide range of other matters. Such activities became increasingly significant in the 1950s and are still of major importance in merchant banking.[7] Spiegelberg's (1973) remarks are still valid[8]:

> No self-respecting sizable merchant bank these days does without a corporate finance department. This is a banking house's Panzer regiment: the troops on whose success and failure, when all is said and done, a merchant bank's reputation rests.

(iv) Activity in the wholesale money markets[9]

In the words of the Wilson Committee[10]:

> The London money markets are the mechanisms by which wholesale funds (mainly short-term) are channelled from lenders to borrowers. They consist of a series of integrated

groups of financial institutions and transactions are conducted primarily by telephone and telex [and increasingly through screen-based systems – DL], there being no physical market place.

On the wholesale money markets participants lend and borrow large amounts at a time – the minimum amount will run into tens of thousands of pounds and the typical sum involved will be five million pounds or more. The wholesale markets can be divided into two. First, there is the traditional money market, known as the 'discount market', where the main participants are banks and 'discount houses' which buy and sell various certificates of indebtedness (for example, 'Treasury Bills', local authority bills, 'Certificates of Deposit' [CDs]). The discount market guarantees liquidity to lenders and borrowers including banks. This market is strictly controlled by the Bank of England; borrowing is short-term (overnight, one week, 90 days) and is always secured against securities like Treasury Bills. Treasury Bills are secure because the United Kingdom Treasury will not default. Second, there are the 'parallel' money markets. Here borrowing, unlike in the discount market, is unsecured. A wide variety of financial institutions, including banks and industrial companies, participate. When borrowing is for periods longer than a year, the term 'capital markets' is sometimes used. The parallel markets can be further divided into sterling and 'eurocurrency' sectors. In the former institutions trade in sterling and in the latter in offshore currencies (eurocurrencies). The markets for 'eurocurrencies', the 'euromarkets', are examined below. British merchant banks and other British financial institutions had not, at the time of the research in 1985, been very successful in the euromarkets[11] although the City was the major centre for these markets.

(v) Investment management

Merchant banks play a crucial role as investment managers of other people's money. They run private clients' departments, they administer and advise pension funds and they operate unit trusts. In the case of pension funds, nearly half the top 24 pension fund managers at the time of the research were well known merchant banks or merchant banking financial groups (including seven members of the Accepting Houses Committee). The smallest amount managed by these top 24 institutions was £980m. S. G.

Warburg, a Merchant Bank which headed the table, controlled £3bn.[12]

(vi) Foreign exchange market

In this market currencies are exchanged 'at rates that fluctuate every minute'.[13] Merchant banks are involved but as relatively small players compared to the likes of Barclays (earnings from the market in 1985: US$113m)[14] or big foreign banks like Citicorp. Merchant banks trade as agents for clients or on their own account, as 'principals'. According to Clay and Wheble, when merchant banks are active in this market:[15]

> Their principal function is to service their customers who are engaged in international foreign trade and investment.

(vii) Venture Capital

In the words of Clay and Wheble,[16] the term 'venture capital' refers to 'investment in new companies with no trading history.' In the last few years merchant banks and other financial institutions have entered this area on a greater scale:[17]

> Stockbrokers, accountants, merchant banks and other financial institutions have been falling over themselves recently to get involved with an industry which is rapidly expanding, which is seen as dynamic and providing a key stimulus to economic revival, and which holds out the prospect of substantial rewards for those that approach the opportunities in the right way.

(b) The Stock Exchange[18]

The Stock Exchange at the time of the fieldwork in 1985 was both a financial market-place and a regulatory organisation. Since then a regulatory body named 'The Securities Association' has taken over the regulatory functions while the financial market side of The Stock Exchange has been drawn into a larger body to form the 'International Stock Exchange'. The remarks below refer mainly to the situation existing at the time of the fieldwork.

The Stock Exchange is a market-place where dealing in stocks and shares takes place. In 1980 the Wilson Committee wrote[19]

> The Stock Exchange is an independent association of stockbrokers and stockjobbers.

Membership at that time was confined to stockbrokers and stockjobbers; banks and other financial institutions and all foreign-owned firms were excluded. As an independent association, The Stock Exchange regulated its activities and those of its members (within the limits of the law) without outside control. The changes associated with Big Bang brought to an end an era in the history of The Stock Exchange in which the Wilson Committee description held true. The fieldwork on which this study is based took place at a time of transition as the City and The Stock Exchange prepared for Big Bang (27 October 1986) but the essential features described by the Wilson Committee remained essentially intact: namely, 'single capacity' and a scale of 'minimum commissions'.

The single capacity system – made obligatory in 1908[20] – stipulated that stockbrokers acted (except in strictly specified circumstances) only as agents for investors or for firms. In other words, stockbrokers bought or sold shares on behalf of clients. Stockbrokers approached jobbers (or as they were more formally named, stockjobbers) who held shares and bought and sold them for profit. Jobbers 'made markets' in stocks and shares. The duty of the stockbroker was to strike deals, at the most advantageous terms, on behalf of their clients.

The second pillar of the pre-Big Bang system was a scale of fixed minimum commissions. Stockbrokers acting as agents earned money by charging a commission when dealing for the client. From 1912 to 1986 a fixed scale of minimum commissions[21] was imposed on stockbrokers. After Big Bang the two pillars of the old system disappeared: member firms are now entitled to act (if they wish) both as agents and market-makers; and negotiated, competitive commissions came into effect. Some stockbrokers, especially the smaller firms, continued after Big Bang to act only in an agency capacity partly through choice and partly because they lack the capital necessary to finance market-making (holding stocks and shares involves capital investment).

In the run-up to Big Bang, many Stock Exchange firms became part of financial conglomerates and lost their former independence as they were bought by banks, insurance companies and other financial institutions. Previously, at most, a minority shareholding was held by other financial institutions.

In a crucial respect The (post-Big Bang and now, International) Stock Exchange has remained unchanged: it is still a market where financial securities are traded. It has changed in that it is now a screen-based market and participants, except for those in the traded options market, work in the dealing rooms of their own firms rather than on a central market floor. The securities traded have always been diverse: interest bearing stocks (company stocks, government issued or guaranteed gilt-edged securities) or shares in the ownership of companies (equities). The market encompasses a 'secondary' market where already issued securities change hands and a 'primary' market where new capital is raised in return for new securities by bodies (for example, industrial companies, the UK Treasury) which wish to expand or finance acquisitions or spending.[22]

At the time of the fieldwork, The Stock Exchange had a second function (post-Big Bang, the two functions of market-place and regulatory body are institutionally separated). In the words of the then (1985) Chairman, Sir Nicholas Goodison[23]:

> The Stock Exchange Council lays down rules and codes of behaviour, organizes the complex business of surveillance to check that people are conforming to the rules and codes, and forces them to do so through an array of disciplinary powers right up . . . to depriving a wrong-doer of his right to carry on his trade.

As explained earlier, this regulatory function is now discharged by The Securities Association.

(c) Euromarkets

In the euromarkets, business is carried out in eurocurrencies. The term 'eurocurrency'[25] is 'used to describe a currency which is held by a depositor in a bank outside the country of origin of that currency'. For example, US dollars held in banks outside the US are known as 'eurodollars'. Eurocurrency markets are dominated by eurodollars but eurosterling, euroyen and so on also play a role. The money advanced to fund loans or buy the various eurocurrency financial instruments (eurobonds, euronotes, eurocommercial paper, and so on) is money held 'offshore' (that is, outside) the national home of the currency. The attraction of the eurocurrency market to investors and others is the lack of regulation by nationally-based authorities of one kind or another, including governments and stock exchange authorities.

The euromarkets, like The Stock Exchange, encompass primary and secondary capital markets. New capital can be raised either by borrowing money (issuing bonds and various other kinds of 'paper', that is, securities) or by selling equity. The euromarkets were already in 1985 much greater sources of new capital than the primary capital market based upon The Stock Exchange. For instance, McRae and Cairncross[26] present figures which demonstrate that these fast-growing markets were even in 1982 a much bigger source of new capital than The Stock Exchange, raising nearly three times as much. Since then the euromarkets have grown spectacularly.[27] London dominates the euromarkets mainly because British governments have exercised so few controls over these financial markets: this free market atmosphere has attracted firms and business to London.

In the euromarkets, financial institutions, governments and industrial companies (and occasional very rich individuals) borrow and lend eurocurrencies, buy and sell newly issued euro-equities (that is, new shares in international companies floated on the euromarkets), trade in second-hand euro-equities, raise money by selling eurobonds or invest in them. Numerous financial instruments are issued and traded: CDs ('Certificates of Deposit' given to investors who deposit funds in a bank; CDs can be traded), syndicated loans, eurobonds, floating rate notes, and so forth. It is not necessary here to understand all the terms associated with these very complex markets but some clarification of key terms is provided.

'Syndicated loans' are loans provided by a syndicate of banks and other financial institutions. Such loans are usually for enormous sums and lending is to top-rated borrowers such as 'blue-chip' corporations (for example, IBM), public authorities and governments. In the hey day of the 1970s, syndicated loans played a key role in recycling the petro-dollars earned by oil-rich states; in the last few years they have declined in importance largely because of the Third World debt crisis.

'Eurobonds' and – a new financial instrument – 'euronotes' had become more significant by 1985. (In the 1970s, syndicated loans became more important and bonds less important.)[28] Eurobonds are securitised (that is, tradeable) forms of debt. The key role of banks as financial intermediaries between suppliers of funds and borrowers is being undermined. Now increasingly corporations, governments, building societies, even banks themselves, issue –

with the help of banks and securities houses (that is, firms such as stockbrokers that issue and deal in securities) – new securities in return for funds rather than borrowing from a bank. Such investors receive securities which they can trade unlike traditional loans (including syndicated eurocurrency loans) which are recorded on certificates and lie passively in the bank's vaults until maturity. Euronotes are a further development of the trend to securitise debt: they are like securitised overdrafts in that the lender can call on the credit lines as they are needed. With a traditional loan, the bank advances money and charges interest which the euronote facility allows the borrower to issue securities as funds are needed. The bank does not normally lend its own funds but 'underwrites' the euronotes: this means that the borrower knows that the necessary funds will be available even if investors are not interested in buying the euronotes at a price acceptable to the borrower – the underwriter guarantees the availability of the required funds.

The markets for eurobonds and euronotes are very complex. In particular, 'swaps' have recently become more popular. Borrowers can arrange to swap interest rates and currencies to cut the costs of borrowing. For example, a corporation may raise US dollars as follows: having a better credit rating in (say) Sweden, the corporation raises the sum needed in Swedish kroner linked to an agreement that the funds can then be swapped for dollars – borrowing costs are lower as a result. Swaps are complicated and require the specialist advice of bankers and securities firms.

Finally, interest rates can be fixed (in market jargon, 'straights') or floating, that is, changed from time to time by reference to an agreed formula. An example of securities with floating rates are FRNs – 'floating rate notes' – or, in market jargon, 'floaters'.

3   RECENT CHANGES IN THE CITY OF LONDON

In the 1980s, change in the City of London has been swift and far-reaching. Two factors, 'deregulation' (or liberalisation) of financial markets and the new information technologies have undermined old City practices. First, 'deregulation' means that old restrictions on competition have been dismantled (for example, foreign firms may belong to The International Stock

Exchange while this was not true for the old Stock Exchange); furthermore, traditional divisions (for example, between stockbroking firm and bank) are altering or disappearing as a result of decisions by various key actors (Department of Trade and Industry, Bank of England, The Council of The Stock Exchange, and the like).[29] In addition, the debt crisis in the Third World has cut lenders off from opportunities which were available in the 1970s and, in consequence, competition between lenders both in the UK and abroad is fiercer than before.[30]

Second, new information technologies have heightened competitive pressures because almost instantaneous connection and dealing with other financial centres all over the world is now possible. 'Global' rather than parochial financial markets are now a reality. Global markets are 24-hour markets because, for example, while London sleeps, Hong Kong is trading. No longer is the City of London protected from outside competition. The most effective competitors in such markets are the enormous international firms, often US and Japanese, which have the capital to span all major financial markets and centres. All these changes – deregulation, new technology, global markets, the rise of giant financial conglomerates – are frequently referred to as the 'City Revolution'. Big Bang in The Stock Exchange is one important aspect of the City revolution.

What were the developments which led up to Big Bang? During the 25 years before Big Bang, The Stock Exchange organised trading around the two separate functions of jobber and stockbroker (the single capacity system). The jobbing system worked well when most investment in terms of value was private investment split up into small parcels. This was still the situation in the early post-Second World War period However, the 'institutional investors' – for example, pension funds, insurance companies and unit trusts – came increasingly to dominate the securities markets. According to Clive Wolman[31]: in 1963, individuals owned 58.7 per cent of shares; in 1975, the proportion was down to 37.5 per cent; by 1984 the percentage had decreased to 22 per cent. Whatever the future may bring – with Conservative and Opposition plans for employee share ownership, forthcoming and proposed privatisation proposals and so on – most dealing in shares and other securities is (and has been for some time) on behalf of institutions which means that, typically, large blocks of shares are traded. However, until Big Bang, the market-makers (the firms of jobbers who bought and sold stocks and shares) were fairly small enterprises which lacked the capital necessary to hold big blocks of securities. As a result, the official or traditional view of dealing diverged from reality. Instead of stockbrokers approaching jobbers with orders which jobbers supplied, increasingly stockbrokers used the 'put through'. The 'put through', involves the stockbroker (not the jobber) finding the counter-party for a large trade (a buyer for a seller and vice versa); prior to Big Bang, the stockbroker was not allowed to act as the market-maker and had to 'put the order through the market'. This involved the jobber as intermediary: the seller had to sell to the jobber and the buyer was obliged to buy from the jobber; in fact the stockbroker did virtually all the work. The stockbroker had to involve the jobber because the single capacity system prohibited stockbrokers from making markets in stocks and shares. Although the jobber had done little (the stockbroker had found the counter-party for the deal), she or he was allowed a profit or 'turn' on the deal. The 'turn' is the profit which results from buying stocks and shares at a lower price than the selling price to ensure a profit. In effect, the jobbing system was breaking down as insitutional domination of the stock market created more and more put throughs.[32]

There was a further pressure on jobbers. One of the justifications of the jobbing system was that market-makers competed on price for business: stockbrokers could strike a deal with the jobber offering the best price for their clients. For various reasons, including the rise of the institutions and inflation, the number of jobbing firms declined steadily to a point where there was little competition in many lines of stock. Figures provided by The Stock Exchange show this trend: 1950, 187 firms; 1960, 100 firms; 1986, 18 firms.[33]

Competition between jobbers also declined in another respect: the decrease in the number of jobbers led to restrictive agreements: for example, jobbers agreed on minimum price spreads between the 'bid' prices at which they bought and the 'offer' prices at which they sold lines of stock. These agreements undermined The Stock Exchange's claim that the jobbing system guaranteed competitive prices.[34]

Increasingly, The Stock Exchange rule book was criticised as a system of restrictive practices. Particular concern was voiced about the exclusion of many types of institutions (banks, insurance companies, foreign firms) from membership and the absence of competition in stockbroking commissions. Institutional investors were incensed by the fact that they had to pay enormous commissions to stockbrokers because commissions were calculated on the value of the deal: a deal for £500 worth of shares for a private client frequently involved as much effort as one for a quarter of a million pounds on behalf of a pension fund; yet, the latter generated much more income for the stockbroking firm. Financial insitutions which were denied membership of The Stock Exchange resented their exclusion from direct dealing with market-makers (Stock Exchange rules forced them to deal with jobbers through the stockbrokers); they knew that in other major world financial centres such restrictions did not exist. The doubts about the anti-competitive aspects of Stock Exchange practice culminated in the decision of the Office of Fair Trading in 1979 to refer the rule book to the Restrictive Practices Court. Matters dragged on until 1983 when Cecil Parkinson, then Secretary of State for Trade and Industry, agreed to a lifting of the case in return for certain concessions by The Stock Exchange. Among these concessions was the acceptance that the scale of minimum commissions should be abolished – this change would both require and enable stockbrokers to compete on price.[35]

Fairly soon after the agreement to scrap minimum commissions, the Council of The Stock Exchange decided that if minimum commissions were to go, then single capacity would also have to be abolished. The reason for this is that the scale of minimum commissions buttressed the single capacity system partly because stockbrokers were guaranteed a decent income (from commissions) and therefore had no incentive to cut out the jobber by making markets and partly because jobbers could not deal directly with clients and merely pay a nominal commission to the stockbroker. Effectively, minimum commissions had subsidised the single capacity system: take away the former and the latter had to go too.[36]

There were other pressures on The Stock Exchange.[37] The rise of global markets necessitated investment in new technologies but Stock Exchange firms were not allowed to raise capital freely from outsiders. Restrictions of this kind curtailed the size of firms.[38] The explosive growth of the euromarkets in which Stock Exchange firms had little involvement allied with the increasing significance of an international market in the securities of large corporations (Glaxo, Beecham, ICI, Jaguar, and so on) threatened The Stock Exchange's position as a major world stock market. Even in London itself the stock market was fragmenting as firms excluded from The Stock Exchange by the old rules dealt 'over-the-counter' in the stocks and shares of leading British and foreign firms.[39] Headlines such as 'Wall Street traders muscle in' (*The Observer*, 31 March 1985), 'Exchange firms face new share dealing rival' (*Guardian*, 12 April 1985), 'Fleming to extend its off-market trading' (*Guardian*, 17 July 1985) indicate the scale of the threat to The Stock Exchange as the central market. The Stock Exchange called upon the Department of Trade and Industry[40] to 'show disapproval of non-Stock Exchange firms who deal in UK securities outside the central market' and stated that it might advance its timetable towards Big Bang (and a more competitive Stock Exchange) to counter the threat. Outside The Stock Exchange there was relatively little sympathy from critics who were relieved that a long-standing virtual monopoly was disappearing. For example, a senior director of one of London's leading merchant banks stated during an interview that The Stock Exchange had been protected for far too long from international competition (he did not refer to restrictions on competition long exercised by merchant banks![41]); in another interview, the head of the London subsidiary of a foreign investment bank referred dismissively to 'The Stock Exchange cartel'.

What about other participants in the City revolution? The changes associated with Big Bang allowed former outsiders to enter The (now, International) Stock Exchange either by joining (for example, Nomura Securities) or by buying up Stock Exchange firms and then applying for membership (for example, Barclays or Mercury, the parent of merchant bank S. G. Warburg). Enormous sums of capital were injected into the UK stockmarket (and other financial markets) as foreign and British-based financial conglomerates geared up for the fight for survival in the new 24-hour, global, information technology-based, deregulated financial markets.[42] Many of the better known (and some of the lesser known) firms of stockbrokers were bought by banks and other institutions. Formerly independent jobbing firms now perform the market-making function as parts of banks or other large financial conglomerates. For example, Morgan Grenfell bought jobber Pinchin Denny and Barclays bought stockbroking firm de Zoete and Bevan and jobbing firm Wedd Durlacher. The new conglomerates provided banking services (merchant and sometimes clearing), agency broking, market-making, insurance, estate agency and a host of other services. The City of London outside the euromarkets is no longer the preserve of relatively small merchant banks and even smaller Stock Exchange firms although many of the small and medium sized stockbroking firms remain agency brokers with no market-making activities. Instead – although smaller firms will remain (for example, merchant bank Barings) in specialist niches – the securities industry in London will be dominated by large conglomerates caught up in a merciless game of competition.

Some quotations and headlines from newspapers in 1985, at the time of the fieldwork, indicate the pace of change in City financial markets:

> Although the Revolution is essentially about reform of the Stock Exchange, the biggest players in it are not stockbrokers but the banks, which are putting together what are likely to be Britain's leading securities broker-dealers for the next several decades, and investing the greatest sums of capital.(*Financial Times*, 7 October 1985).[43]

> Swiss bank buys into Phillips & Drew (The latter being a leading stockbroking firm) (*Financial Times*, 6 November 1984).

> Samuel Montagu to buy full control of Greenwell (the former being one of the City's leading merchant banks and the latter the top stockbroking firm in the Gilt-edged securities markets) (*Financial Times*, 25 February 1985).

> Chase Manhattan, the third largest bank in the U.S., is to form a U.K. securities group by acquiring two London stockbroking firms . . . (*Financial Times*, 27 November 1984).

> Barclays de Zoete Wedd (BZW), the new securities group being assembled by Barclays Bank for the City Revolution will be launched next year with a net asset value of £200–220m . . . (*Financial Times*, 10 May 1985).

> U.S. group to buy jobber (*Financial Times*, 12 June 1985).

Morgan makes markets, and makes them work for international investors (Advertisement by *The Morgan Bank*, *Financial Times*, 18 July 1985).

Finally, the new framework of investor protection must be mentioned. The Financial Services Act 1986 laid the basis for a new regulatory system in the financial sector to regulate dealings in securities and the activities of insurance companies, unit trusts and other participants in financial markets.[44] The reforms concluded a protracted debate in which Professor Gower played a key role. The new system is a more formal system, based on statute, than that which previously regulated financial markets. City regulatory bodies were previously often inadequate at policing their markets and some major scandals both forced the government to act and City leaders to accept what would have been fiercely and successfully resisted only a decade before.

The aim of the new legislation and accompanying framework of City controlled self-regulatory bodies is to achieve more effective policing of financial markets at a time of unprecedented change. First, it is now an offence to carry on an investment business without authorisation. Second, the Department of Trade and Industry has delegated its power under the Financial Services Act 1986 to SIB (Securities and Investments Board), an independent body. SIB supervises a number of SROs (Self-Regulatory Organisations), each of which is responsible for particular spheres or financial markets. The rules of SROs must be approved by SIB. Third, authorisation to engage in business may be provided either by the overall regulatory body, SIB or in most cases by SROs. Finally, the new provisions make a distinction between Investment Exchanges and SROs. Investment exchanges are organised financial markets such as The International Stock Exchange, the over-the-counter market, and so on. Each is subject to a particular regulatory body (for example, The Securities Association regulates the Stock Exchange). Overall, both the financial markets and the regulatory structure of the City are subject to more detailed and systematic control than ever before.

4 BASIC FINANCIAL MARKET TERMS

This section clarifies important terms and is of particular

relevance for reading chapter 3.[45] Technical terms or expressions will normally only be explained on their first appearance. The terms covered are (a) 'principals' and 'agents'; (b) 'dealing'; (c) 'taking a position' and 'running a book'; (d) 'making markets'; (e) 'hedging' and 'speculation'.

(a) 'Principals' and 'Agents'

A 'principal' deals on her or his own account and not as an 'agent' for another. The Stock Exchange before Big Bang, when single capacity was obligatory, provides a good example of the distinction. Jobbers were principals and stockbrokers were agents. A jobbing firm bought and sold stocks and shares on its own account using the firm's capital and not the capital of a client. The firm earned income by buying and selling at a profit. If a jobber bought 250 000 shares at 100 pence and sold them at 102 pence, the profit belonged to the jobbing firm. Stockbrokers under single capacity were (except under certain strictly defined circumstances) obliged to act as agents: stockbrokers bought and sold for clients and acted, therefore, as intermediaries who were expected to arrange the best possible deal for clients. In the post-Big Bang stock market firms may act in both capacities, as market-makers or as agency stockbrokers.

The distinction between principals and agents is applicable in other financial markets (and in other markets, such as, commodity markets for tea and rubber). For example, a bank may buy US dollars from another bank for its own use: in this case it acts as a principal. However, on other occasions, it may buy foreign currency on behalf of corporate or private clients: here it acts as an agent. Agents are referred to as 'brokers': for example, foreign exchange brokers, stockbrokers, insurance brokers and so on. The broker acts on behalf of a client, seeking the best terms for the client whether the client be buying, selling, borrowing or lending.[46] For example, a bank may use a foreign currency broker, who charges a commission, to find the cheapest terms for buying US dollars. The financial relationship between the buyer and the seller of dollars is mediated by a broker. The bank pays the broker commission because it believes that overall using a broker is more profitable than acting on its own behalf. Those who deal in foreign currency (buying and selling US dollars, Japanese yen, and so on) sometimes use brokers but are not obliged to do so. (Most of the restrictions on direct dealing between banks in the foreign currency markets were lifted in 1979.)[47]

(b) 'Dealing'

One is said to be 'dealing' when one agrees to buy and sell at a specific price or on particular terms. Dealing is the conclusion of a process of information seeking and bargaining. The deal may involve, for example, the purchase or sale of a financial instrument (shares in a company, eurobonds) or a foreign currency. One may deal as agent or principal. Individuals whose professional function is actually to carry out the bargaining and conclude the deals are referred to as 'dealers'. Dealers work on market floors or, increasingly, in the dealing rooms of a firm. the dealing room is a hive of modern communications technology while market floors, like The Stock Exchange at the time of the research, rely on traditional face-to-face methods combined with new technology. Dealing rooms existed before the new communications technology came to predominate but in the old days the telephone and, even earlier, the telegraph were the major means of communication with counter-parties.

(c) 'Taking a position' and 'running a book' (also 'short' and 'long' positions)

Principals deal from their own 'books'; the 'book' being a record of what one holds in each line of stock, currency and so on. A firm acting as a principal deals on its own account and in the securities markets is said to be 'running a book'. If the firm buys shares or Swiss francs, say, it 'takes a position'. 'Taking a position' means that the firm has invested capital (sometimes City practitioners talk about 'putting money up-front') and is consequently exposed to the movement of the market. For example if the firm uses US dollars to buy deutschmarks on the assumption that the deutschmark will appreciate against the dollar, so that it may end up (after buying dollars back) with more dollars than before, it has 'taken a position': that is, it has invested money and is now exposed to the market. It will gain or lose depending upon whether its view of how the market will develop is correct or not: in market jargon, the firm has 'taken a view' and taken a position on the basis of that view.

The expression 'running a book' relates to the fact that the firm which is buying and selling as a principal notes down all transactions in a 'book' (in the past, literally a book; now 'books' are held in computers) and is thereby able to see the 'position' of the dealing desk or firm at a glance. In any institution which deals as a principal, someone, often a junior of some sort (a 'positions clerk' in a foreign exchange dealing room or a trainee jobber on the market floor of pre-Big Bang Stock Exchange), will have responsibility for keeping a note of all deals. The record allows the firm to keep track of its holdings and, to determine what prices the dealers should 'make' to attract business and generate profits or, at least, contain losses. The prices the firm makes – whether it be buying or selling – depend upon what it holds or is short of as well as its view of the market. Because it makes a great deal of its profits by dealing it is forced to make competitive prices. Here is an example. A dealing room does business in securities or foreign exchange. If the firm holds the securities or currency it has a 'long position'; if it sells whatever it deals in without owning it, intending to buy before the delivery date, it has a 'short position'. A firm which expects the prices of what it deals in to rise will prefer to have a long position and, correspondingly, if it expects prices to fall will prefer a short position.

(d) 'Making markets'

A principal in any market buys from those who wish to sell and sells to those who wish to buy: it is said to be 'making a market' in the particular item. A firm which 'makes markets' will 'make' (or 'quote') a 'two-way price' for every item: it makes both a 'bid' (its buying) price and an 'offer' (its selling) price. A market-maker agrees to be available on as continuous basis as possible to counter-parties: to act as a seller to a potential buyer and vice versa. Market-makers are not committed to deal both ways at all times. Even when a market-maker is unwilling to deal both ways, it will make a two-way price. In these circumstances, when told that the other is a seller (or buyer) or is acting for a seller (or buyer), the firm will state that it is trying to do business the 'same way'. For example, a bank may be asked for 'cable' (the US dollars-sterling exchange rate) and provide a two-way price but when told that the other wants to buy US dollars, may refuse to deal, the dealer saying 'same' meaning that the bank also needs dollars. In this case the bank may have sold dollars short and require dollars for delivery to the buyer; or the firm may be wishing to buy dollars now in anticipation of an appreciation of the dollar against sterling.[48]

(e) 'Hedging' and 'Speculation'

A firm is 'hedging' when it acts to protect investments against price changes. Imagine that a firm in charge of particular investment funds (acting as a 'fund manager') knows that £2 million will be available for investment in a week but fears that the market will rise sharply before then. The fund manager can protect the capital in various ways: for example, by using 'traded options'.[49] 'Traded options' give the holder the right to buy ('call options') or sell ('put options') a particular company's shares (the 'underlying shares') at a guaranteed price (the 'striking price') on or before a specified date. The price of traded options depends upon the striking price, the underlying share price and the length of time before the traded options contract expires. Our fund manager hopes to buy 50 000 ICI shares when the money becomes available. She buys call contracts for a small (relative to the share price) premium and these guarantee the right to buy the shares at an acceptable price in a week's time. If the shares do not rise during the week, the small premium may have been lost but the value of the capital has been protected in return for a small stake. If the shares do rise, the fund manager buys the shares at the striking price which is below the new higher market price. In fact, even if the shares fail to rise, the traded option contracts are worth something up to expiry and may be sold to recoup some of the premium.

A 'speculator' takes a view of the market and invests not primarily to protect capital but to make gains as the market moves. Investors can 'speculate' in securities, currencies, commodities and so on. The traded options market is used here as an example. The speculator buys traded option contracts in the hope that the price of the traded option concerned will rise in line with an anticipated rise in the underlying share price. For example, ICI rose from 984 pence to 1004 pence at one point in July 1986. Let us assume our speculator had bought October call options at a striking price of 950 pence. As a result of the rise of the underlying share price, the October 950 call options rose 12 pence from 70 to 82 pence, a gain of more than 17 per cent in two days. This is the end that a speculator always has in mind although it is only achieved sometimes because market movements frequently disappoint the speculator.

5 KEY SPECIALIST FUNCTIONS AT THE TIME OF THE FIELDWORK (1985)[50]

Several functions need clarification in addition to those already discussed. The essentials are summarised in Figure A3.1.

(a) Specialists in Stockbroking Firms

At the time of the fieldwork, Stock Exchange firms were organised around the distinction between agents (stockbrokers) and principals (jobbers). The following explanation of terms refers to that (pre-Big Bang) period only in order to avoid an unnecessary complexity.

Every stockbroking firm had dealers who were in direct contact with the jobbers: these dealers collected prices from jobbers and struck deals on behalf of clients. The dealer acted on instructions from the 'institutional salesmen' (usually called 'salesmen') or the 'private clients' department. The salesmen were in contact with fund managers in the institutions (for example, pension funds, unit trusts, insurance companies): fund managers instructed the salesmen to buy and sell on their behalf. However, salesmen were not passive: they offered advice to institutional clients and fund managers and tried to persuade them to carry out certain deals. The dealing business of private investors passed, not through the salesmen on the institutional sales desk, but through the private clients department.

Both private clients' specialists and institutional salesmen depended upon the advice of investment analysts (usually just called 'analysts'). Each analyst specialises in particular sectors (for example, food manufacturers or banks). Robert Sobel's description[51] of the Wall Street analyst applies also to the City of London both in 1985 and today: like an investigative reporter on a newspaper, the analyst's work involves research, interviewing and detection. The analyst follows the effect of general economic trends on the industry, examines the accounts of individual firms,

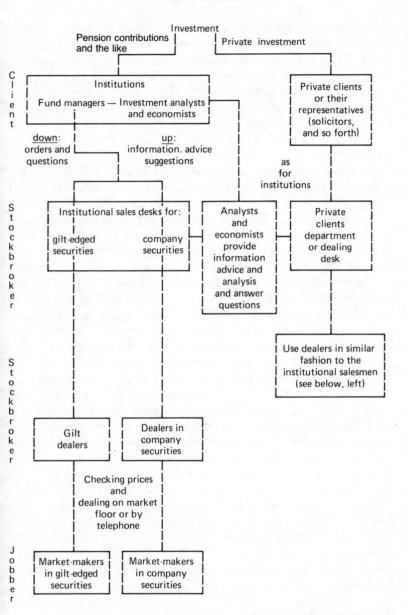

FIGURE A3.1   *The Dealing Chain* (at time of fieldwork, 1985)

visits firms and keeps an eye on news about the industry. The analyst is especially keen to spot trends in the prices of stocks and shares before others or anomalies in the price (for example, the price may be on the low side given the firm's current prospects and performance). When the analyst has something to communicate, she or he writes a circular which always leads to a precise conclusion.[52] 'We forecast that the profit of this company will be X' and concludes with a simple injunction: 'Buy' (or 'Sell' or 'Hold').

Analysts and salesmen observed and interviewed during the research were in an intensely competitive environment. Fund managers who had money to invest were in contact with numerous stockbroking firms. Salesmen had to persuade fund managers to take their advice seriously and to use the dealing facilities of their firm. Analysts aimed to provide the salesmen, or the institutional clients directly, with good quality information and reliable predictions about market trends.[53] A former fund manager told the researcher that most circulars from analysts in stockbroking firms went straight into the bin; favoured salesmen and analysts were given direct telephone lines to the fund managers in this insurance company while others went through a switch board. This seemed a common arrangement.

The bigger stockbroking firms also employed technical staff such as economists, accountants, computer experts and statisticians. Like merchant banks, many stockbroking firms contained individuals specialising in venture capital and corporate finance. The latter has always been regarded as particularly prestigious because it involves frequent contact with leaders of major corporations and involvement in high level decision-making.

Finally, there were many specialists, normally working at a lower level in the hierarchy, in the 'back offices' of firms –who provided essential administrative support, including the processing of contract notes after deals were struck on behalf of clients. Back office staff were not interviewed except for three who held managerial or partner (that is, ownership) status.

(b) Specialists in Jobbing Firms

Jobbing firms encompassed fewer specialist divisions. Increasingly in the last years before Big Bang, they employed statisticians and computer specialists but, on the whole, those in career posts either actually made markets or (if senior) managed. It is interesting that some of the most senior managers were actually involved closely in the dealing process. For example, a director might spend his day on the market floor rather than back at the office.

(c) Fund Managers

In the investing institutions, broad decisions about investment policy were made by the directors of the firm (say, the merchant bank) in co-operation with the investors (say, pension fund trustees). Lower down fund managers made investment decisions on a day-to-day basis, often after discussion with senior staff. Fund managers took investment decisions about a particular block of money but usually within parameters decided by the investors or the directors or partners of the firm. Fund managers are found in stockbroking firms, unit trusts, merchant banks, clearing bank (for example, NatWest) unit trust departments, investment trusts, in the pension fund departments of some industrial firms and in specialist investment management firms. Usually, fund managers had served an apprenticeship as analysts. Fund managers had the benefit of the advice of in-house analysts as well as those based outside.

(d) Private Clients Departments (in stockbroking firms and merchant banks)

Private clients still account for a big slice of investment. Frequently, private clients are advised to invest in unit trusts, often those managed by the particular firm. Otherwise, especially in the case of wealthy individuals, their money is managed on a discretionary basis (especially if they are very rich) or a non-discretionary basis (especially if they are not very rich). 'Discretionary' means that the stockbroker or merchant banker or investment manager may buy or sell without consulting the client. Private clients' specialists manage the 'portfolios' of their clients and this includes advice on taxation and insurance requirements.

6 THE STOCK EXCHANGE HIERARCHY AT THE TIME OF THE FIELDWORK

Trainee dealers, whether stockbrokers or jobbers, were formally called 'unauthorised clerks' and informally 'blue-buttons'. After passing an examination in the relevant practical skills, blue-buttons became 'authorised clerks'. Authorised clerks were usually referred to as 'dealers' whether they worked for jobbing or stockbroking firms. The next step up was to pass the full Stock Exchange Examination to qualify for membership of The Stock Exchange. 'Associate Members' were members of The Stock Exchange who were either self-employed or fairly senior staff who had not (sometimes, not yet) achieved partner or management status.

NOTES

1. United Kingdom Department of Trade and Industry, *Financial Services in the United Kingdom: A new framework for investor protection*, para. 1.1.
2. The following references were particularly useful: H. McRae and F. Cairncross, *Capital City*: pp. 49–63; W. M. Clarke, *Inside the City* pp. 10–13, 21–2, 47–8, 223–4; Wilson Committee, *Report*; C. J. J. Clay and B. S. Wheble, *Modern Merchant Banking*; surveys published by the *Economist* and *Financial Times* as specified below. Taped interviews with merchant bankers provided information about each individual's own duties and the activities of merchant banks as a whole.
3. See note 2 for references. Many brochures and advertisements issued by the merchant banks visited were consulted – in both the variety of activities is obvious. The banks cannot be identified for reasons of confidentiality.
4. Wilson Committee, *Report*: paras. 3.52–3.56.
5. See, for example: *The Economist*, 'International Investment Banking: a Survey', 16 March 1985: pp. 34 and 39.
6. W. M. Clarke, *Inside the City*: p. 269.
7. Plender, *The Square Mile*: pp. 67–8; McRae and Cairncross, *Capital City*: pp. 60–1; Spiegelberg, *The City*: chapter 3.
8. Spiegelberg, *The City*: p. 68.
9. This section is based upon a reading of the financial press, especially the *Financial Times*. Other references include: G. Bannock *et al.*, *The Penguin Dictionary of Economics*: pp. 124–5; McRae and Cairncross, *Capital City*: pp. 73–84; Wilson Committee, *Appendices*, Appendix 3: chapter XV; Clarke, *Inside the City*: chapters 8 and 14.
10. Wilson Committee, *Report*: para. 195.

11. See, for example, P. Ferris, *Gentlemen of Fortune*: p. 173; McRae and Cairncross, *Capital City*: p. 145.
12. *Financial Times*, Table of 'Leading Pension Fund Managers', 25 February 1986.
13. Clarke, *Inside the City*: p. 172.
14. *Financial Times* Survey, 'Foreign Exchange', 27 May 1986.
15. Clay and Wheble, *Modern Merchant Banking*: p. 80.
16. Clay and Wheble, *Modern Merchant Banking*: p. 67.
17. *Financial Times* Survey, 'Venture Capital', 28 November 1984: p. 1.
18. This discussion draws upon the financial press, especially the *Financial Times*. In addition, the following references were used: Clarke, *Inside the City*: chapter 5; J. Dundas Hamilton, *Stockbroking Today*: chapters 1–4 and 7; J. Dundas Hamilton, *Stockbroking Tomorrow*: chapters 1–5; McRae and Cairncross, *Capital City*: chapter 6; Wilson Committee, *Report*: chapter 7 and *Appendices*: Appendix 3: chapter XIV; several publications of The Stock Exchange: for which, see Bibliography. A brief survey of the changes in the stock market since 1985 us to be found in S. M. Yassukovich, 'The International Stock Exchange – What It Means For Companies' (pp. 18–20) in *Interchange*, Summer 1987.
19. Wilson Committee, *Appendices*: Appendix 3: chapter XIV para. 3.293.
20. E. Victor Morgan and W. A. Thomas, *The Stock Exchange*: p. 146.
21. Morgan and Thomas, *The Stock Exchange*: pp. 153–4.
22. See, for example: Wilson Committee, *Report*: paras. 187–94; Wilson Committee, *Second Stage Evidence*, Vol. 4: p. 6 (Written evidence of The Stock Exchange to the Committee).
23. Sir Nicholas Goodison, 'The Regulation of Financial Services in the United Kingdom', *The Stock Exchange Quarterly*, March 1985.
24. The following sources have been particularly useful: Plender, *The Square Mile*: chapter 2; Clarke, *Inside the City*: chapter 14; J. Coakley and L. Harris, *The City of Capital*: chapter 3. In addition: see the following *Financial Times* Surveys, 'International Capital Markets', 18 March 1985; 'World Banking', 7 May 1985; 'International Capital Markets', 17 March 1986; 'World Banking': Part 1, 22 May 1986; *Economist*, 'International Investment Banking: A Survey', 16 March 1985. A major weakness of Stock Exchange firms before Big Bang was their virtual absence from the booming euromarkets: see for instance, B. Riley, 'A Snub for the Stock Exchange', *Financial Times*, 19 October 1985.
25. S. Valentine *International Dictionary of the Securities Industry*: p. 67.
26. McRae and Cairncross, *Capital City*: p. 145.
27. Plender, *The Square Mile*: p. 27.
28. See: Plender, *The Square Mile*: pp. 35–7. See the following *Financial Times* Surveys: 'World Banking', 7 May 1986: p. 5; 'International Capital Markets': 18 March 1985, p. 8.
29. 'Deregulation' in the sense of removing inhibitions or restrictions on competition has gone hand in hand with the construction of a new system of investor protection.
30. Plender, *The Square Mile*: pp. 24–5.
31. C. Wolman, 'Wider Share Ownership', *Financial Times*, 11 January 1986. See also: Clarke, *Inside the City*: chapter 6; McRae and Cairncross, *Capital City*: chapter 5; Coakley and Harris, *The City of Capital*: chapter 5; and for

major institutional holdings in 1982–84, *The Stock Exchange Quarterly*, March 1986, Appendix 3.

32. Clarke, *Inside the City*: pp. 76–7; Plender, *The Square Mile*: pp. 80–6; McRae and Cairncross, *Capital City*: pp. 137–44. The Stock Exchange *Code of Dealing*: chapter 2, section C regulàted the conduct of 'put through' business in some detail.

33. The Stock Exchange, *The Stock Exchange Quarterly*, March 1986, Appendix 4.

34. Plender, *The Square Mile*: p. 83.

35. Hamilton, *Stockbroking Tomorrow*: pp. 10–16; Sir N. Goodison, 'The Stock Exchange at the Turning point', *The Stock Exchange Quarterly*, March 1985, pp. 7–11.

36. Wilson Committee, *Report*: para. 342; Plender, *The Square Mile*: p., 97.

37. This discussion of the City Revolution draws upon the following references in addition to others specifically mentioned later: The Lex Column, 'Trading equities across borders', *Financial Times*, 5 August 1985; A. Nicoll, 'Round-the-clock trading brings a new challenge', *Financial Times*, 5 November 1985; B. Riley, 'The cast is assembled, but may change in rehearsal', *Financial Times*, 28 December 1986; Anon., 'All change in the City', *The Economist*, 7 December 1985; McRae and Cairncross, *Capital City*: pp. 143–4 and chapter 10; Plender, *The Square Mile*: pp. 75–86.

38. For a brief outline of the Stock Exchange response to this problem, see: Goodison, 'The Stock Exchange at the Turning Point', *The Stock Exchange Quarterly*, March 1985, pp. 7–8.

39. The OTC ('over-the-counter' market) operated outside the regulatory structure of The Stock Exchange. In the OTC firms deal from their own 'book' (see below) and, before the new Financial Services Act and the associated comprehensive structure of regulation of the securities industry, investors lacked the protection of both single capacity dealing and the Stock Exchange rule book. Some OTC firms were reputable but others were engaged in dubious practices of various kinds including systematic milking of private investors (institutions were better able to take care of themselves).

40. J. Moore, 'SE plea sparks securities talks', *Financial Times*, 3 April 1985.

41. See, for example, M. C. Lisle-Williams, 'A Sociological Analysis of Changing Social Organization and Market Conduct in the English Merchant Banking Sector' (University of Oxford D. Phil. thesis, 1982): chapter 5, section 2 and p. 74.

42. See, for example: D. Lascelles, 'The stampede to become global players', *Financial Times*, 2 April 1986; Lascelles, 'Global wrestling match hots up', *Financial Times*, 11 April 1986. L. C. B. Gower *Review of Investor Protection*: Part 2, para. 1.08 concisely summarises the background to, and the main elements of, the changes in The Stock Exchange.

43. D. Lascelles, 'In better shape to ring the changes', in *Financial Times* Survey, 'UK Banking', 7 October 1985.

44. See: Wilson Committee, *Report*: chapter 22 and para. 1411; L. C. B. Gower, *Review of Investor Protection: Report*: Part 1, chapters 1-7 and Part II, chapters 2–4; U.K. Department of Trade and Industry, *Financial Services in the United Kingdom: A new framework for investor protection*; J. Moore and

others, feature on the Financial Services Bill, *Financial Times*, 20 December 1985. M. Clarke (*Regulating the City*: chapter 4) outlines recent developments in the stock market, discusses some significant scandals and examines the debate about regulating the city which accompanied the preparations for Big Bang. Finally, press coverage was a useful source on the progress of discussions in Parliament and the City about the new regulatory framework.

45. The explanation of terms is based on information collected in over a hundred interviews, conversations with participants in, and observation of, financial markets, daily reading of the financial press over a long period (including detailed supplements about financial markets published in the *Financial Times* and *Economist*) and various books. Books consulted were: Clarke, *Inside the City*: esp. Glossary; Valentine, *International Dictionary of the Securities Industry*; Bannock, *The Penguin Dictionary of Economics*; Cummings, *Investor's Guide to the Stock Market*; D. G. Hanson, *Dictionary of Banking and Finance*; N. Stapley, *The Stock Market: A guide for the private investor*; J. Rowlatt, *A Guide to Saving and Investment*; various publications of The Stock Exchange including the *Code of Dealing* (see Bibliography for other Stock Exchange publications).

46. Wilson Committee, *Report*: para. 94.

47. Wilson Committee, *Report*: para. 3.37.

48. This explanation of practice in the foreign exchange market is based on conversations and interviews with dealers and a positions clerk in the dealing room of a small investment bank. In addition, notes made during an interview with a foreign exchange broker proved valuable.

49. This discussion is based upon three days of observation of the traded options market. Two individuals were interviewed and many other participants talked to the writer. In addition, reference was made to Stock Exchange publications: *Traded 'Puts'*; *Call Options in Action; A Simple Guide to Traded Options; Introduction to Traded Options*. Other useful publications include: Cummings, *Investor's Guide to the Stock Market*: pp. 23–7; Stapley, *The Stock Market*: Section 13.2; Rowlatt, *A Guide to Saving and Investment*: pp. 121–4.

50. This section relies on interviews and conversations with more than a hundred individuals; in many cases participants in the markets provided detailed descriptions of their work tasks.

51. R. Sobel, *Inside Wall Street*: p. 133.

52. Example provided by interviewee (Taped interview: 225).

53. On analysis see: W. Hopper, 'The Stockbroker' in R. Fraser (ed.), *Work*, ii; especially pp. 274–6.

Bibliography

Anon, 'All change in the City', *The Economist*, London 7 December 1985.

Bannock, G., Baxter, R. E. and Rees, R., *The Penguin Dictionary of Economics* (3rd edn) (Harmondsworth: Penguin, 1984).

Bassett, P., 'Doctors head non-manual pay league with £400 average', *Financial Times*, 30 October 1985.

Beer, S., *Modern British Politics* (new edn) (London: Faber & Faber, 1982).

Bendix, R., *Max Weber: An intellectual portrait* (London: Methuen, 1966) (reprinted 1973).

Beveridge, W., *Full Employment in a Free Society* (2nd edn, 2nd impression) (London: Allen & Unwin, 1967).

Boyson, R. (ed.), *1985: An Escape from Orwell's 1984* (Enfield, Middlesex: Churchill Press, 1975).

Burgess, R. G. (ed.), *Field Research: a Sourcebook and Field Manual* (London: Allen & Unwin, 1982).

Burgess, R. G., *In the Field: An Introduction to Field Research* (London: George Allen & Unwin, 1984).

Checkland, S. G., 'The Mind of the City, 1870–1914', *Oxford Economic Papers*, ix, 1957, pp. 261–78.

Clarke, W. M., *Inside the City: a guide to London as a financial centre* (revised edn) (London: Allen & Unwin, 1983).

Clarke, M., *Regulating the City* (Milton Keynes: Open University Press, 1986).

Clay, C. J. J. and Wheble, B. S., *Modern Merchant Banking* (2nd edn, revised by L. H. L. Cohen) (Cambridge: Woodhead-Faulkner, 1983).

Coakley, J. and Harris, L., *The City of Capital* (Oxford: Basil Blackwell, 1983).

Committee to Review the Functioning of Financial Institutions (Chairman: Sir Harold Wilson), *Second Stage Evidence*, iv (London: HMSO, 1979).

Committee to Review the Functioning of Financial Institutions (Chairman: Sir Harold Wilson), *Report* (Cmnd. 7937) (London: HMSO, 1980) (reprinted 1983).

Committee to Review the Functioning of Financial Institutions (Chairman: Sir Harold Wilson), *Appendices* (Cmnd. 7937) (London: HMSO, 1980) (reprinted 1983).

Crick, B., *Socialist Values and Time* (Fabian Society Tract No. 495) (London: Fabian Society, 1984).

Crosland, C. A. R., *The Future of Socialism* (abridged and revised paperback edn) (London: Jonathan Cape, 1964).

Cummings, G. *Investor's Guide to the Stock Market* (3rd edn) (London: Financial Times Business Information, 1984).

Dalton, G., *Economic Systems and Society: Capitalism, Communism and the Third World* (Harmondsworth: Penguin, 1974) (reprinted 1977).

Denzin, N., *The Research Act: a theoretical introduction to sociological methods* (2nd edn) (New York: McGraw-Hill, 1978).

Donaldson, P., *10 x Economics* (Harmondsworth: Penguin, 1982).

Donaldson, P., *A Question of Economics* (Supplementary material by R. Moore) (Harmondsworth: Penguin, 1985).

Economist, The, 'International Investment Banking: A Survey', *The Economist*, 16 March 1985.

Fabian Society (Meacher, M. *et al.*, *Social Security: The Real Agenda* (Fabian Society Tract No. 498) (London: Fabian Society, 1984).

Ferris, P., *The City* (London: Victor Gollancz, 1960).

Ferris, P., *Gentlemen of Fortune: The World's Merchant and Investment Bankers* (London: Weidenfeld & Nicolson, 1984).

Financial Times Survey, 'Venture Capital', *Financial Times*, 28 November 1984.

Financial Times Survey, 'International Capital Markets', *Financial Times*, 18 March 1985.

Financial Times Survey, 'World Banking', *Financial Times*, 7 May 1985.

Financial Times, Table of 'Leading Pension Fund Managers', *Financial Times*, 25 February 1986.

Financial Times Survey, 'International Capital Markets', *Financial Times*, 17 March 1986.

Financial Times Survey, 'Foreign Exchange', *Financial Times*, 27 May 1986.

Financial Times Survey, 'World Banking', Part 1, *Financial Times*, 22 May 1986.

Friedman, M., *Capitalism and Freedom* (Chicago: University of Chicago Press, 1962) (14th impression, 1975).

Friedman, M. and Friedman, R., *Free to Choose* (Harmondsworth: Penguin, 1980).

Gamble, A., 'The Free Economy and the Strong State' in Miliband, R., and Saville, J. (eds), *The Socialist Register 1979* (London: The Merlin Press, 1979).

Gamble, A., 'Economic Policy' in Drucker, H., Dunleavy, P., Gamble, A. and Peele, G. (eds), *Developments in British Politics* (revised and updated) (Basingstoke: Macmillan, 1984).

Gamble, A., *The Free Economy and the Strong State* (Basingstoke: Macmillan, 1988).

Geisst, C. R., *A Guide to the Financial Markets* (London: Macmillan, 1982) (reprinted 1984).

George, V. and Wilding, P., *Ideology and Social Welfare* (London: Routledge & Kegan Paul, 1976).

Gilmour, I., *Inside Right: Conservatism, Policies and the People* (London: Quartet, 1978).

Gilmour, I., *Britain Can Work* (Oxford: Martin Robertson, 1983).

Glaser, B. G. and Strauss, A. L., *The Discovery of Grounded Theory: Strategies for Qualitative Research* (Chicago: Aldine, 1967).

Goodison, Sir N., 'The Regulation of Financial Services in the United Kingdom', *The Stock Exchange Quarterly*, March 1985.

Goodison, Sir N., 'The Stock Exchange at the Turning Point', *The Stock Exchange Quarterly*, March 1985.

Gough, I., 'State Expenditure in Advanced Capitalism', *New Left Review*, 92, July–August 1973.

Gough, I., *The Political Economy of the Welfare State* (London: Macmillan, 1979).

Gower, L. C. B., *Review of Investor Protection, Report*: Part 1 (Cmnd. 9125) (London: HMSO, 1984) (reprinted 1985).

Gower, L. C. B., *Review of Investor Protection, Report*: Part 11 (London: HMSO, 1985).

Hall, S., *The Hard Road to Renewal: Thatcherism and the Crisis of the Left* (London: Verso, 1988).

Hamilton, J. Dundas, *Stockbroking Today* (2nd edn) (London: Macmillan, 1979).

Hamilton, J. Dundas, *Stockbroking Tomorrow* (Basingstoke: Macmillan, 1986).

Hammersley, M. and Atkinson, P., *Ethnography: Principles in Practice* (London: Tavistock, 1983).

Hanson, D. G., *Dictionary of Banking and Finance* (London: Pitman, 1985).

Harris, N., *Beliefs in Society* (London: Watts, 1968).

Harris, R. and Seldon, A., *Over-Ruled on Welfare* (Hobart Paperback No. 13) (London: Institute of Economic Affairs, 1979).

Harrison, A., 'Economic Policy and Expectations' in Jowell and Airey (eds) [1984].

Hayek, F. A., *The Road to Serfdom* (London: Routledge & Kegan Paul, 1944) (reprinted 1979).

Hayek, F. A., *The Constitution of Liberty* (London: Routledge & Kegan Paul, 1960) (reprinted 1976).

Hayek, F. A., *Law, Legislation and Liberty* (with corrections and revised Preface) (London: Routledge & Kegan Paul, 1982).

Heath, A., Jowell, R. and Curtice, C., *How Britain Votes* (Oxford: Pergamon, 1985).

Hodgson, G., *The Democratic Economy* (Harmondsworth: Penguin, 1984).

Hopper, W., 'The Stockbroker' in Fraser, R. (ed.), *Work*, ii (Harmondsworth: Penguin, 1969).

Huhne, C., 'The new Conservative myth about the workshy of Britain', *Guardian*, 10 October 1985.

Ingham, G., *Capitalism Divided?: The City and Industry in British Social Development* (Basingstoke: Macmillan, 1984).

Jowell, R. and Airey, C. (eds) [1984], *British Social Attitudes: the 1984 report* (Aldershot: Gower, 1984).

Jowell, R. and Witherspoon, S. (eds) [1985], *British Social Attitudes: the 1985 report* (Aldershot: Gower, 1985).

Jowell, R., Witherspoon, S. and Brook, L. (eds) [1986], *British Social Attitudes: the 1986 report* (Aldershot: Gower, 1986).

Jowell, R., Witherspoon, S. and Brook, L. (eds) [1987], *British Social Attitudes: the 1987 report* (Aldershot: Gower, 1987).

Lascelles, D., 'Global wrestling match hots up', *Financial Times*, 11 April 1986.

Lascelles, D., 'In better shape to ring the changes' in *Financial Times* Survey of 'UK Banking', *Financial Times*, 7 October 1985.

Lascelles, D., 'The stampede to become global players', *Financial Times*, 2 April 1986.

Lex Column, The, 'Trading equities across borders', *Financial Times*, 5 August 1985.

Linton, M., 'Cracks show in Tory convictions', *Guardian*, 4 October 1985.

Lisle-Williams, M. C., 'A sociological analysis of changing social organization and market conduct in the English merchant banking sector' (University of Oxford D. Phil. thesis, 1982).

Lisle-Williams, M. C., 'Beyond the market: the survival of family capitalism in the English merchant banks', *British Journal of Sociology*, xxxv: No. 2, June 1984, 241–71.

Lisle-Williams, M. C., 'Merchant banking dynasties in the English class structure: ownership, solidarity and kinship in the City of London, 1850–1960', *British Journal of Sociology*, xxxv: No. 3, September 1984, 333–62.

Lloyd, J., 'Surge in City earnings "set to continue"', *Financial Times*, 31 July 1985.

Lupton, T. and Wilson, C. Shirley, 'The Social Background and Connections of "Top Decision Makers"' in Urry, J. and Wakeford, J. (eds), *Power in Britain* (London: Heinemann Educational Books, 1973).

MacRae, H. and Cairncross, F., *Capital City: London as a Financial Centre* (2nd edn) (London: Methuen, 1984).

Mann, M., *Socialism can Survive: Social Change and the Labour Party* (Fabian Society Tract No. 502) (London: Fabian Society, 1985).

Mann, M., 'Work and the Work Ethic' in Jowell, Witherspoon and Brook (eds) [1986].

Mannheim, K., *Ideology and Utopia* (London: Routledge & Kegan Paul, 1960) (reprinted 1966).

Manning, D. J., *Liberalism* (London: Dent, 1976).

Marx, K. and Engels, F., *The German Ideology* (London: Lawrence & Wishart, 1965).

Miliband, R., *The State in Capitalist Society* (London: Weidenfeld & Nicolson, 1969).

Mill, J. S., *Principles of Political Economy* (edited by Winch, D.) (Harmondsworth: Penguin, 1970).

Mills, C. Wright, *Power, Politics and People* (edited by Horowitz, I. L.) (New York: Oxford University Press, 1967).

Mishra, R., *The Welfare State in Crisis: Social Thought and Social Change* (Brighton: Wheatsheaf, 1984).

Miller, A., *Death of a Salesman* (Harmondsworth: Penguin, 1961) (reprinted 1970).

Moore, J. *et al.*, Feature on the Financial Services Bill, *Financial Times*, 20 December 1985.

Moore, J. 'SE plea sparks securities talks', *Financial Times*, 3 April 1985.

Morgan, E. Victor and Thomas, W. A., *The Stock Exchange* (2nd edn) (London: Elek, 1969).

Nicoll, A., 'Round-the-clock trading brings a new challenge', *Financial Times*, 5 November 1985.

Nove, A., *The Economics of Feasible Socialism* (London: Allen & Unwin, 1983).

Oakley, A., *Subject Women* (New York: Pantheon 1981).

Office of Population Censuses and Surveys, *Classification of Occupations 1980* (Government Statistical Service) (London: HMSO, 1980).

Owen, D., *Face the Future* (London: Jonathan Cape, 1981).

Owen, D., *A Future That Will Work* (Harmondsworth: Penguin, 1984).

Parekh, B., 'How not to be a Thatcherite', *New Statesman & Society*, 16 December 1988.

Parkin, F., *Marxism and Class Theory* (London: Tavistock, 1979).

Parkin, F., 'Strategies of Social Closure in Class Formation' in Parkin, F. (ed.), *The Social Analysis of Class Structure* (London: Tavistock, 1974).

Peacock, A. T. and Wiseman, J., *The Growth of Public Expenditure in the United Kingdom* (revised 2nd edn) (London: Allen & Unwin, 1967).

Phillips, P., *YAPS: The complete guide to Young Aspiring Professionals* (London: Arrow, 1984).

Plamenatz, J., *Ideology* (London: Macmillan, 1971).

Plant, R., *Equality, Markets and the State* (Fabian Society Tract No. 494) (London: Fabian Society, 1984).

Plender, J., *The Square Mile* (London: Century Hutchinson, 1985).

Pym, F., *The Politics of Consent* (London: Hamish Hamilton, 1984).

Riley, B., 'The cast is assembled, but may change in rehearsal', *Financial Times*, 28 December 1986.

Riley, B., 'A snub for the Stock Exchange', *Financial Times*, 19 October 1985.

Robinson, J. and Eatwell, J., *An Introduction to Modern Economics* (Maidenhead: McGraw-Hill, 1973).

Rowlatt, J., *A Guide to Saving and Investment* (5th edn) (London: Pan, 1984).

Jessop, Bob, 'The Transformation of the State in Post-war Britain' in Scase, R. (ed.), *The State in Western Europe* (London: Croom Helm, 1980).

Schumpeter, J., *Capitalism, Socialism and Democracy* (3rd edn) (New York: Harper & Row, 1962).

Scott, J., *The Upper Classes: Property and Privilege in Britain* (London: Macmillan, 1982).

Sharpe, S., *'Just Like a Girl': how girls learn to be women* (Harmondsworth: Penguin, 1976).

Shils, E., *The Constitution of Society* (Chicago: University of Chicago Press, 1982).

Smith, C. W., *The Mind of the Market* (New York: Harper Colophon, 1983).

Smith, M., 'Further state sales lined up', *Guardian*, 18 July 1985.

Sobel, R., *Inside Wall Street* (New York: W. W. Norton, 1982).

Social Democratic Party, *Newsletter*, No. 1, April 1981.

Spencer, H., *The Man Versus The State* (Indianapolis: Liberty Classics, 1981).

Spiegelberg, R., *The City: Power without accountability* (London: Quartet, 1973).

Stapley, N. F., *The Stock Market* (2nd edn) (Cambridge: Woodhead-Faulkner in association with Laing and Cruickshank, 1984).

Steel, D. and Holme, R. (eds), *Partners in One Nation* (London: The Bodley Head, 1985).

Stimson, G. V., 'Place and space in sociological fieldwork', *The Sociological Review*, 34: No. 3, August 1986, 641–56.

Stock Exchange, The, 'Appendix 3' and 'Appendix 4' *The Stock Exchange Quarterly*, March 1986.

Stock Exchange, The (Information and Press Department), *Call Options in Action* (London: The Stock Exchange, n.d.).

Stock Exchange, The, *Code of Dealing* (London: The Stock Exchange, January 1985).

Stock Exchange, The (Information and Press Department), *The Gilt Options* (London: The Stock Exchange, n.d.).

Stock Exchange, The (Information and Press Department), *The Gilt-Edged Market* (London: The Stock Exchange, n.d.).

Stock Exchange, The (Information and Press Department), *The Index Options* (London: The Stock Exchange, n.d.).

Stock Exchange, The (Information and Press Department), *An Introduction to Buying and Selling Shares* (London: The Stock Exchange, n.d.).

Stock Exchange, The (Information and Press Department), *Introduction to Traded Options* (London: The Stock Exchange, n.d.).

Stock Exchange, The (Information and Press Department), *A Simple Guide to Traded Options* (London: The Stock Exchange, n.d.).

Stock Exchange, The (Information and Press Department), *The Stock Exchange* (London: The Stock Exchange, n.d.).

Stock .Exchange, The (Information and Press Department), *Traded 'Puts'* (London: The Stock Exchange, n.d.).

Tawney, R. H., *The Acquisitive Society* (London: Fontana, 1961).

Tawney, R. H., *Equality* (London: Allen & Unwin, 1964).

Tawney, R. H., *The Radical Tradition* (Harmondsworth: Penguin, 1966).

Tawney, R. H., *The Attack and Other Papers* (Nottingham: Spokesman, 1981).

Taylor-Gooby, P., 'Citizenship and Welfare' in Jowell, Witherspoon and Brook (eds) [1987].

Trades Union Congress, *TUC SUMMARY of an Opinion Poll carried out for the TUC by NOP Market Research on PRIVATISATION AND PUBLIC OWNERSHIP* (London: Trades Union Congress, n.d.).

Trades Union Congress, *Stripping Our Assets: The City's Privatisation Killing* (London: Trades Union Congress, 1985).

United Kingdom Cabinet Office, *Lifting the Burden* (Cmnd. 9571) (London: HMSO, 1985).

United Kingdom Department of Trade and Industry, *Financial Services in the United Kingdom: A new framework for investor protection* (Cmnd. 9432) (London, HMSO, 1985).

Valentine, S., *International Dictionary of the Securities Industry* (London: Macmillan, 1985).

Vickers, J. and Yarrow, G., *Privatisation and the natural monopolies* (London: Public Policy Centre, 1985).

Weber, M., *The Methodology of the Social Sciences* (New York: The Free Press, 1949) (reprinted 1969).

Weber, M., *The Protestant Ethic and the Spirit of Capitalism* (London: Allen & Unwin, 1930) (11th impression, 1971).

Weber, M., *Economy and Society*, i (edited by Roth, G. and Wittich, C.) (Berkeley: University of California Press, 1978).

Wedderburn, D., 'Theories of the Welfare State' in Miliband, R. and Saville, J. (eds), *The Socialist Register 1965* (London: Merlin Press, 1965).

Westergaard, J. and Resler, H., *Class in a Capitalist Society* (Harmondsworth: Penguin, 1976).

Whitley, R., 'The City and Industry: the directors of large companies, their characteristics and connections' in Stanworth, P. and Giddens, A. (eds), *Elites and Power in British Society* (Cambridge: Cambridge University Press, 1974) (reprinted 1975).

Williams, R., *Keywords: A Vocabulary of Culture and Society* (Glasgow: Fontana/Croom Helm, 1976).

Williams, R., *Marxism and Literature* (Oxford: Oxford University Press, 1977).

Williams, S., *Politics is for People* (Harmondsworth: Penguin, 1981).

Wilson Committee: see 'Committee to Review the Functioning of Financial Institutions'.

Wolman, C., 'Wider Share Ownership', *Financial Times*, 11 January 1986.

Yassukovich, S., 'The International Stock Exchange – What it Means for Companies', *Interchange* (London: The Stock Exchange) Summer 1987.

Young, K., 'Shades of Opinion' in Jowell and Witherspoon (eds) [1985].

Index